The Chaos Factory

The inside story of corporate IT failure.

Adam Zachary Wasserman

 Epimetheus Press

FIRST EDITION, JUNE 2019

The Library of Congress has catalogued this edition as follows:
Wasserman, Adam Zachary.
The Chaos Factory: The inside story of corporate IT failure. / Adam Zachary Wasserman. – 1st ed.

ISBN: 978-1-9992423-0-5

Book design by Adam Z. Wasserman

Printed in the United States of America
10 9 8 7 6 5 4 3 2 1

For my wife and children
who believed in me and supported me,
and my mother and my aunt
who read and edited,
and in memory of my uncle
who was an example to me my entire life.

Three things are certain:

Death, taxes, and lost data.

Guess which has occurred.

~ David Dixon 1998

Winning entry of the
Haiku Error Messages 21st Challenge
by Charlie Varon and Jim Rosenau,
sponsored by Salon.com

Preface

Even though software is something that affects everyone, almost no one really understands how it is made. Most people wonder why many large companies, with all of the resources at their disposal, cannot seem to make a website or mobile application that is reliable and easy to use.

I am an insider. I have spent thirty years managing software development for companies large and small. I mostly love my job, but I must admit that there is one aspect of it that has been extremely unpleasant.

The failure rate of government and corporate IT projects is unacceptably high. Over the past twenty-three years, barely a third of Information Technology (IT) projects are considered successful by the executives responsible for them[1]. They are consistently late, over budget, or "crippled", which is to say functionally incomplete or sometimes even unusable. The human cost of this failure in terms of despair and stress is incalculable.

But there is hope. Broken industries can be fixed. When I was 12 years old in 1975, family road trips were inevitably accompanied by mechanical trouble. Fan belts broke, radiators boiled

---

[1] *The Chaos Report*. The Standish Group International, 1994-2017

over. Once or twice the car actually caught fire. Really.

This sounds pretty dramatic today, but anyone my age or older will have vivid recollections of similar automotive disasters. My dad cursed his car back then as much as you curse your computer today. The entire American automobile industry collapsed in 2008 in great part because of a decline in sales due to a lack of quality.

Today it is possible to buy a car that you can drive at seventy miles per hour for twenty-four hours straight without a single blip. Mile after mile, year after year, modern cars perform safely, reliably, and dollar for dollar, much more cost-effectively than they did forty years ago, or even ten years ago.

Another example would be furniture. People used to have to save for months or even years to get a dining room or bedroom set. Now you can go to Ikea and buy a very handsome set for one week's salary. It begs the question: why can't we make developing an application as predictable and reliable as manufacturing a car or as easy to assemble as an Ikea table?

Over the years, I have devoted a lot of thought and a lot of real-world experimentation to getting at the root cause of this failure. I have adopted methodologies, been certified a few times in a few things, and I have invested myself heart and soul into making the world of software development better and more productive for both the people that make the software, and the people that use it.

This book is the culmination of all these years of effort, and I am surprised to see how obvious the cause of IT project failure seems in retrospect:

Industrial scale production requires industrial methods, *but IT does not use industrial methods.*

With this book I invite you, the reader, into my world. I hope that the examples I give and the explanations I provide will give you a "peek behind the curtain" to appreciate a rich and complex history of which very few people are aware.

But even more, I hope that this book will give business managers and shareholders the arguments they need to cut through the endless excuses that IT departments use to explain why they cannot meet entirely reasonable demands to do better.

"Simplicity is a great virtue but it requires hard work to achieve it and education to appreciate it. And to make matters worse: complexity sells better."

~ Edsger Dijkstra

Table of Contents

"Should array indices start at 0 or 1? My compromise of 0.5 was rejected without, I thought, proper consideration."

~ Stan Kelly-Bootle

Part Zero

Where I answer the questions: Why should you read this book? Will this book be a bunch of gobbledygook? Does this book apply to all software development? How many parts are there in this book, and what does each part cover?

Why should you read this book?

Software applications affect almost everybody alive. Yet almost nobody really understands how they are created. Many people have a vague sense that things could be much better than they are, but there is an impenetrable wall of technical jargon and plausible excuses that surrounds every poorly performing application.

Failure of IT application development projects is the norm. By failure we mean over budget, over schedule, or non-functional to one degree or another. In study after study, year after year, well-respected industry analysts report that the business people who fund IT projects consider only a third of them to be successful.

One solution after another has been tried since these failures first started to be noticed in 1988. None of them have worked.

Project Management in particular, held itself out as the cure for all ills. Not only has it failed to make things better, it actually makes things worse. I will explain exactly how.

Current production methods for software are pre-industrial. Nobody expects a software development project to succeed without master programmers. And although everybody accepts this as normal, it is anything but normal. People trust their lives every day to cars that were assembled by high school graduates (and in some cases high school dropouts), not master engineers. The way applications are developed today is very similar to the way cars were assembled in the very early 1900's, and it cannot scale to the level of demand that exists today. There are simply not enough master programmers. If you are not sure what I mean by this, and why it is a problem, don't worry. The middle part of this book is dedicated to simply and clearly explaining the whole thing.

Industrial Production is a proven means of leveraging master talent in such a way that a scalable, unskilled or semi-skilled workforce can be used to achieve mass production. Again, if this means nothing to you now, don't worry. I will explain exactly how this can be done.

Will this book be a bunch of gobbledygook?

No.

My book is written for the non-technical reader: the business manager who would like to understand "how we got to this place" and "what can we do about it". It is written for shareholders who intuitively feel that something is not right but lack the technical vocabulary to express what common sense is telling them. Or anybody at all who has wondered why some darned website won't work right!

I want to entertain you, give you a peek into a world that is vitally important to your day-to-day life, yet mysterious, hidden, and mostly unknown. I also think that I can give you a basic understanding of programming. Enough for you to decide for yourself whether you believe what I say in this book or not.

Even though I am a professional, I still feel the same sense of frustration that you do when I go the web site or mobile application a bank, telco, or airline, and am confronted with a confusing, broken, application that I cannot make heads or tails of. Information Technology (IT) professionals have lots of explanations to give you as to why things are so bad, but those explanations are often as confusing and frustrating as the applications themselves, and there is a simple reason for that: if IT executives and managers *really* knew what was wrong, not only could they explain it, they could have fixed it a long time ago.

So, what we hear from them are not really explanations; they are *excuses*. You are not going to get excuses from me.

Does this book apply to all software development?

No.

Although all apps are software not all software is an app. There is software in cars, airplanes, microwave ovens, and assembly line robots. That kind of software usually does not have a graphical user interface or allow end-users to manipulate data, two things common to almost all apps. This book is not about that kind of software.

As well, there are technology companies whose apps are their entire business: the "FANGs" (Facebook, Amazon, Netflix, and Google) and other similar companies such as Uber, eBay, YouTube, Kayak, and any business whose *only* business is to create mobile or web-based apps for customers to use. The software they write is not a *project*, it is their *product*, and it is *not* written by their IT department. Their IT department's job is to run the office network.

Application development is the main business activity of these companies, and they go about the process very differently than a telephone company, bank, or manufacturer does. They hire differently, they pay different salaries. They have a different culture and different working conditions. They have different processes for specifying or defining apps, different ways of deciding upon and approving funding for development. This book is not written for or about these companies.

A government or corporate IT department has about as much in common with the development teams at a FANG as a giraffe does with a rhinoceros. I do not expect a government or corporate IT department to successfully apply the culture and practices that make a technology company work, nor do I expect anything I say to apply to these technology companies.

This book is about the most un-sexy of subjects: mass production. If you look at how many customer self-service payment portals there are, or how many electronic storefronts there are, or even how many separate web-based applications a single Fortune 500 company has, we are definitely in mass-production territory.

Increasingly, apps are a competitive *necessity* for companies. People's choice of which telephone company to use or television provider to subscribe to is more often than not significantly (if not entirely) influenced by the quality of the experience provided on the web and in mobile applications. It is not even uncommon for people to select their banks based upon the quality of the apps the bank provides. And a bad website can cause a potential customer to immediately seek an alternative supplier.

I am going to tell you all about *that* kind of application.

How many parts are there in this book, and what does each part cover?

Part One gives an overview of the evolution of computing and programming from a highly personal point of view. I included it for the entertainment and education of the reader who would like to learn about the basics of programming before reading my analysis of where things have gone wrong.

It is definitely not required reading, and if you feel you already know everything you need to know about programming you can skip right over it. If you do read it, please bear in mind that I leave a lot out. There are over 2,500 programming languages, a complete history of programming would have to be at least 2,500 pages long. I only talk about a handful of the programming languages that have been most used by corporate IT departments.

My goal is to give you just a smattering of the principles, history, and culture of programming. To give you an overall sense of things so that you can better judge for yourself the argument I make in Part Four. But I have done my very best to be entertaining.

Part Two starts in 1990 and describes a perfect storm of different forces that converged at the end of the millennium to create the system of application development used by most companies today; a system that does not work.

In particular I describe how IT project management tried to take over the world, and explain exactly why it makes things worse, even though it is supposed to make things better.

Part Three is a short (about a thirty-minute read) history of manufacturing. As with Part One, it is from a highly personal perspective, carefully researched with citations, but by no means comprehensive. I focus on only the aspects that are significant because they are applicable to the problem of IT project failure.

Part Four is where I make my case that IT has not yet been industrialized, and exactly how that causes project failure.

I will then present how I believe industrialization will be achieved.

The conclusions are uncomfortable and unwelcome to IT specialists who are deeply invested in the status quo, but they have been immediately recognized as simple common sense by every non-specialist with whom I have ever discussed them.

"If debugging is the process of removing bugs, then programming must be the process of putting them in."

~ Edsger W. Dijkstra

Part One

A history of programming: how it has been affected by languages, methodologies, and by the computer hardware itself.

Chapter One
The Metal years: 1950-1960

In the Beginning...

...there were no programmers, because the computers *were the program*. They did not really resemble modern computers in any way. They weighed tons and took up whole walls in rooms with custom-built air conditioning and ventilation for their relays and tubes, not to mention specially reinforced floors.

Long before I learned how to program; in fact, quite a long time before I was born, the first computers were "programmed" by flipping electro-mechanical switches and plugging in wires on a patch panel.

The people (wearing lab coats) who operated these computers didn't even think of the plugging and switch flipping as "programming" any more than you think you are programming when you setup your DVR to record your favorite show, or when you reheat your lunch in the microwave. The program was designed by electrical engineers and built into the wiring of these incredibly expensive giant electric calculators. What these people were doing was *entering the problem* to be calculated.

The photo below is often mis-labeled *Programming the ENAIC computer*. The fact is that like all other computers of its time, ENIAC was *not programmable*. What made it special however, was that instead of having just one program hardwired into it, it had many. Each one of the panels you see in the photo was one hardwired program. Using patch cables computer operators could configure the panels together to run one program/panel from the results of another. It required a great deal of creativity and expertise and was groundbreaking in its own right. Nonetheless, it was simply not programming as you and I understand the term (sitting at a computer screen, writing algorithms in a programming language).

Computer operators configuring ENIAC

Although Konrad Zuse is now recognized as having been first to invent the modern *programmable* computer and the first programming language, as a scientist ion Nazi Germany his efforts remained top secret for a long time. The thing that really launched software programming as we know it today was the publication of the *First Draft of a Report on the EDVAC*[1] in 1945, written (or perhaps more accurately: assembled and edited) at the request of the U.S. Army by John Von Neumann, a remarkable fellow, with enough achievements to take up an entirely different book than this one. The report described the basis for modern computers as we know them; binary calculators that execute programs in machine language that have been stored in some kind of memory. Therefore, EDVAC *wasn't hardwired* for any programs. Programs had to be written using opcodes (which I will describe soon a few pages from here) and loaded at *runtime*. Circulation of this report is undeniably the catalyst for modern computer design.

In 1949 EDVAC ran its first program, read from a gigantic roll of magnetic tape. The tape spools were so massive that my mother

---

[1] Von Neumann, John. "First Draft Of A Report On The EDVAC". 1945, *Moore School Of Electrical Engineering, University Of Pennsylvania,* doi:10.5479/sil.538961.39088011475779.

was discouraged from entering the field for fear it was not possible for a woman to physically transport them to and from the computer.

It was 1949: Harry Truman became president and introduced his *Fair Deal*, it was the first year in which no African-American was reported lynched in the United States of America. Canadians and Australians broke free of the commonwealth and created their own citizenships. Mao and the People's Republic of China took power. Israel held its first election and joined the UN. The German Democratic Republic was established. NATO was formed. Winston Churchill proposed the European Union. The first non-stop around-the-world airplane flight succeeded, the first jet powered airplane flew, the Soviet Union tested its first atomic bomb, and computer programming was born.

Where a calculator on the ENIAC is equipped with 18,000 vacuum tubes and weighs 30 tons, computers in the future may have only 1,000 vacuum tubes and weigh only 1(and)1/2 tons.

~ Popular Mechanics, March 1949

Then there was the word

"Von Neumann" computers, as modern computers are sometimes called, all operate on some basic shared principles. They have random access memory (RAM) divided into two spaces called the stack and the heap. The heap is used to store the running program, and the stack is used to store the data that is the input and output. As you will see later, some clever programmers play tricks, hiding data within code, or code within data.

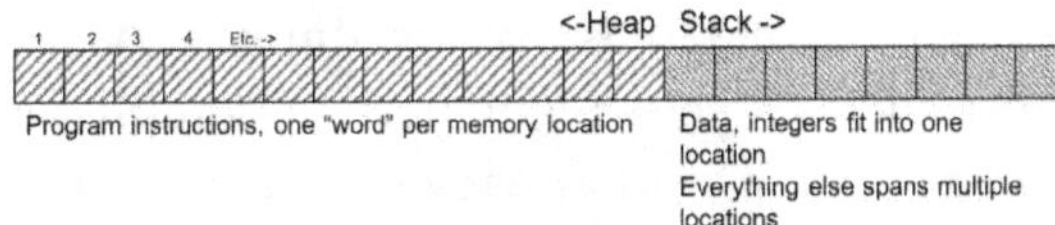

A binary[2] program is stored in the heap as a series of hexadecimal *words*[3], which are fed to the Central Processing Unit (CPU) one at a time. Words are different lengths on different CPUs. Very old CPUs used 8-bit words, modern CPUs use 64-bit words. Each word triggers a specific CPU *operation*. For this reason, they are called *opcodes*. For example, on an old

---

[2] You can learn about binary on YouTube: https://youtu.be/lsCKJ6se_1w, and about bits and bytes at https://youtu.be/b7pOcU1xMks

[3] Whereas our familiar counting system is base 10 and binary is just base 2, a hexadecimal system is base 16.

16-bit Intel CPU, the hexadecimal (a way of shortening binary numbers) opcode "2104" will store the number from stack location 104 to a special scratchpad in the CPU called a *register*. "1105" will add the number from stack location 105 to the first number and "3106" will take the result and store it in stack location 106. *All* computer programs, no matter what language the programmer uses, eventually come down to a series of *words* stored in memory.

In *assembly language*, a three-letter mnemonic represents a single binary or hexadecimal machine instruction. For almost a decade, programmers exclusively used assembly language to locate and retrieve data in memory and move it to the CPU for computation. The step by step instructions do not really resemble normal human logic in any way.

Below is a very simple program that adds two numbers. I show the binary, the hex, and the assembly instructions side by side (the data is not shown).

Binary	Hex	Assembly	Description
0010	2104	LDA 104	Get data from
0001			memory location
0000			104
0100			

Binary	Hex	Assembly	Description
0010 0001 0000 0101	1105	ADD 105	Add data from memory location 105
0010 0001 0000 0110	3106	STA 106	Store result in memory location 106

Here is a simple assembly language program that prints out the phrase "Hello World". The first words on lines 5-9 are examples of opcodes (there are other opcodes in this program that are not as easily pointed out).

```
1    section .text
2    global _start
3    _start:
4                    ; write our string to stdout.
5    mov    edx,len  ; third arg: message length
6    mov    ecx,msg  ; second arg: pointer to msg
7    mov    ebx,1    ; first arg: file handle (stdout)
8    mov    eax,4    ; system call number (sys_write)
9    int    0x80     ; call kernel
10                   ; and exit.
11   ebx,0           ; first syscall argument: exit code.
12   mov    eax,1    ; system call number (sys_exit)
```

```
13    int    0x80        ; call kernel.
14    section .data
15    msg db "Hello, world!",0xa ; the string to print.
16    len equ $ - msg             ; length of the string.
```

This kind of programming is called *bare metal* programming[4]. The code is terse and hard to understand. It had to be small because the capacity of computers was small.

The cellphone that you likely have in your pocket has 30 million times more storage and is about 10 million times faster than an IBM 650 was in 1954. The smallest program on your cell phone would not fit on 10,000 IBM 650s wired together. The phone hardware is also about 40,000 times smaller and lighter, uses about 400,000 times less power, and is 10,000 times less expensive. The IBM 650 cost half a million dollars in 1954 which is equal to about 4.6M today.

For the rest of Part One, I will describe the technological advances that allowed programmers to evolve ever larger and increasingly more complex programs.

---

[4] http://www.catb.org/jargon/html/B/bare-metal.html

Speaking in tongues

In 1957, FORTRAN (FORmula TRANslation) made it possible for people to write programs by composing with human language and logic instead of difficult to remember opcodes.

The way human readable programming languages work is by taking a concept, such as printing out something, which as we saw just above takes a dozen lines of assembly code and *abstracting*[5] that concept into one *reserved word*. Reserved words are not the same as binary or hexadecimal words. Reserved words are human language code words that represent whole sentences in computer words. In the case of FORTRAN the reserved word that substitutes for the assembly program above is "write".

A special program called a *compiler* expands "write" into the sixteen lines of assembly language, and other reserved words into their respective assembly language equivalents.

As we shall soon see, many early programmers didn't like compilers. They did not trust them to do as good a job as a human. In the very beginning there may well have been merit

---

[5] I will provide am in depth explanation of what *abstraction* means in computing later on, in Chapter Four.

to that, but over the years, humans transferred a lot more of their "smarts" into compilers. Also, as computer capacity got larger, the programs got a lot larger and more complex. It would be almost impossible for a modern programmer to beat a compiler, and almost nobody even tries.

But in the old days, even when they used a compiler, programmers were still "close" to the metal. They usually knew what the compiler was doing, what "choices" it would make when it "saw" certain patterns in the human readable language. Good programmers would write their human readable code in specific ways meant to force the compiler into "doing the right thing".

Here is the "Hello World" program in FORTRAN:

```
implicit none

write ( *, '(a)' ) 'Hello, world!'

stop

end
```

As you can see, writing in FORTRAN reduced the number of programming statements required. On the average by a factor of twenty.

The increase in programming productivity was an order-of-magnitude because the longer or more complex a program is, the more signif-icant the productivity gain becomes. The ex-amples I give you are very short. With a larger program (tens of thousands of lines) the differ-ence is much more dramatic. Writing five hun-dred lines instead of ten thousand is a lot more impressive than writing four instead of sixteen.

A few years earlier, Grace Hopper had created a language for business use called FLOW-MATIC, based on her belief that peo-ple should be able to program a computer using plain English and have the computer convert the English words into machine instructions for itself. Few people have heard of FLOW-MATIC, but many people have heard of COBOL (COmmon Business Oriented Lan-guage) which was based in very large part upon FLOW-MATIC and was considered by many to be more human readable than FORTRAN.

```
IDENTIFICATION DIVISION.
PROGRAM-ID. HELLO-WORLD.
* simple hello world program
PROCEDURE DIVISION.
    DISPLAY 'Hello world!'.
    STOP RUN.
```

It must be said that COBOL is disliked by many programmers for being extremely wordy.

The MIT Jargon File[6] has this to say:

COBOL fingers /koh'bol fing'grz/ n.

Reported from Sweden, a (hypothetical) disease one might get from coding in COBOL. The language requires code verbose beyond all reason (see candygrammar); thus it is alleged that programming too much in COBOL causes one's fingers to wear down to stubs by the endless typing. "I refuse to type in all that source code again; it would give me COBOL fingers!"

Nevertheless, making programming accessible to a greater number of people constituted a productivity improvement on the whole, and it was still a lot less code than assembly.

Just about every language in common use today is a descendant not of FORTRAN or COBOL, but of two other influential languages came into being at the same time, LISP, which is sometimes still used today for

---

[6] "The Jargon File is a glossary and usage dictionary of computer programmer slang. The original Jargon File was a collection of terms from technical cultures such as the MIT AI Lab, the Stanford AI Lab (SAIL) and others of the old ARPANET AI/LISP/PDP-10 communities, including Bolt, Beranek and Newman, Carnegie Mellon University, and Worcester Polytechnic Institute". https://en.wikipedia.org/wiki/Jargon_File

The whole text is available at http://catb.org/jargon/html/index.html.

I read it with religious fervor when I was in my *larval stage*. You can look up *larval stage* in the Jargon File.

Artificial Intelligence (AI) programming, and ALGOrithmic Language (ALGOL). Just about every language in common use today is a descendant not of FORTRAN or COBOL, but of ALGOL (sometimes with a little LISP influence thrown in for good measure). But those descendants would only start to appear twenty years later.

The next decade belonged to the computer manufacturers and the electrical engineers. They would improve programming productivity not through languages, but through hardware and operating systems.

"Here is a language so far ahead of its time, that it was not only an improvement on its predecessors, but also on nearly all its successors."[7]

~ Sir Charles Antony Richard Hoare
(Turing award winning computer scientist speaking about ALGOL)

---

[7] C. A. R. Hoare. 1973. *Hints on Programming Language Design*. Technical Report. Stanford University, Stanford, CA, USA.

Chapter Two
Big iron: 1960-1970

When dinosaurs roamed the earth[1]

The first computers cost millions of dollars in their day, the equivalent of tens of millions today. The corporations that made them sold only a few dozen a year. Both the computers themselves, called mainframes, and the companies that made them were gigantic, slow, lumbering beasts. And programming was a slow lumbering task.

Prior to the seventies, programmers did not code directly "on a computer" the way they do today. Programmers wrote or typed code by hand. It was then converted to 3 and ¼-inch tall punch cards by data entry clerks (or sometimes by the programmers themselves). Each punch card was one line of a program, and God help the programmer whose card deck got

---

[1] **dinosaur:** n.

Any hardware requiring raised flooring and special power. Used especially of old minis and mainframes, in contrast with newer microprocessor-based machines. In a famous quote from the 1998 Unix EXPO, Bill Joy compared the liquid-cooled mainframe in the massive IBM display with a grazing dinosaur "with a truck outside pumping its bodily fluids through it". IBM was not amused. Compare *big iron*; see also *mainframe*.
http://www.catb.org/jargon/html/D/dinosaur.html

knocked over or dropped because only the most expensive keypunch machines numbered the cards as they were produced.

Programmers invented all sorts of tricks to prepare for the sad day they would suffer this fate. Notice the diagonal lines drawn in marker on the edges of the cards below. If (or more usually, when) someone dropped the stack of cards, the diagonal would help a little bit in getting them lined up and back in the proper order.

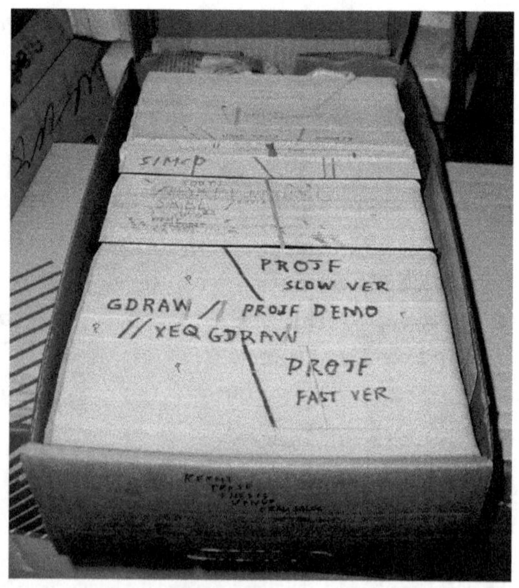

Once the cards were re-sorted – and the dirty looks dispensed with – the programmer would request some time on the computer and submit the batch of punch cards to a queue (The box above is a queue. Not that fancy, huh?).

During peak times, it was common to stand in line waiting to submit a batch of cards. Sometime later (hours or even days) a computer operator would run the program, and a printout of the results would be returned to the programmer along with the punch cards. If there were no results, or if there were errors, the programmers would read over their code looking for bugs and compare it to the punch cards to see if a typographical error had been made on the keypunch.

Many early productivity improvements were simply advances that reduced the cycle time in this process. Eventually punch cards became obsolete.

Mainframe computer manufacturers such as Rand/Sperry, IBM, Burroughs, and Honeywell would create an operating system (OS) for every new computer model they brought to market. An operating system is a special program that controls the hardware and provides hardware access to all the other programs that run on the computer.

In 1964, some productivity gain was made with the introduction of the IBM System/360 computer series with its OS/360 operating system. This series of computers was the first to offer *interoperability* among all computers in the series by means of a common operating system. This meant that a program written on one model of computer could be run on any other computer in the series without needing to be rewritten or recompiled. This in itself was a major gain in productivity, but it also allowed programmers to test code on relatively inexpensive machines that it was easier to get time on. Once the code was right it could be moved to more expensive, larger capacity computers.

System 360 was also a popular computer (along with the Digital Equipment PDP-10) for *time-sharing services*. Time-sharing service bureaus would use banks of teletype machines to allow multiple programmers to enter their programs simultaneously, and then send them via modem to a mainframe computer to be executed using "spare cycles", moments when the CPU was not being used by higher priority jobs.

This was the very beginning of interactive programming. However, it was still nothing like today. There were electric typewriters instead of screens, a response time of ten seconds was considered blazingly fast, and it was not unusual to have to wait minutes or hours to see the results of a program. Still it was a dramatic improvement over punch cards.

Although the System/360 introduced the IBM 2250 video display terminal (VDT) that used a cathode ray tube (CRT) the teletype terminal remained far more popular. One has only to look at the price of the 2250 to see why. It cost over a quarter of a million dollars *for one display*. That is close to two million dollars in today's money and was equal to the cost of the System/360 computer itself. It was not until the late 1970's that the cost of VDTs became low enough for them to replace teletypes.

In my opinion, the most lasting contribution of System/360 to the world was Fred Brooks' book, The *Mythical Man Month*. But that book would not appear until a decade later, so you'll have to wait for me to tell you more about it in chapters to come.

Smaller, faster, better

In 1965 an upstart company named Digital Equipment Corporation introduced a *minicomputer* called the PDP-8. It was *mini* because it was *only* as large as refrigerator. It also had a mini price. One could buy a dozen PDP-8s for the same price as one System/360. That meant that a dozen programmers could each have a "dedicated" computer to work on, and that people who had never before had access to a computer, now did. The PDP-8 was followed by the PDP-10, which as I mentioned, was instrumental in the creation of timesharing and also was the backbone of the research project that eventually became the Internet, which in turn created the hacker communities.[2] Many famous names in computing today got their start on a time-sharing service.

At the end of the decade, an era was drawing to a close. The giant computer manufacturers were on the edge of a precipice they could not see. Minicomputers and personal computers (PCs) were about to change the world. Hardware design had up until this time been a recognized science and career for electrical engineers while programming was a sideline that people with real careers (such as math or physics) engaged in out of personal interest. But this changed with the emergence of the discipline of computer science, which was focused on programming and software as the engine of innovation. Software would eventually become more important than hardware, and two men

---

[2] http://www.catb.org/jargon/html/T/timesharing.html

who were among the most influential in this regard were Donald Knuth and Edsger Dijkstra.

Programming comes of age

I regret to say, I will not write much about
Knuth here. He is truly one of the most influential minds in the history of computer science,
but his work is rarefied, highly mathematical,
and inaccessible to anyone without an extensive and very solid understanding of the language of mathematics. Personally, it takes me
a day to read one page of his *The Art of Computer
Programming*, and Volume One (of seven) was
2000 pages long. You may have guessed: I
never finished it. Heck, even Knuth never finished it! After 50 years, he has only published
up to the first part of Volume Four of seven
planned volumes. His work did much to legiti-
mize computing and advance it as a science,
however in my very humble opinion, he did not
play much of a role in advancing the *productivity*
of programming, which is what this book is
about.

Dijkstra was a Dutch physicist and mathematician who quite simply fell in love with
programming. Afraid to leave the respectable
career of physicist to pursue what was considered by most to be a hobby, Dijkstra was per-
suaded by his boss, a mathematician who had

abandoned an academic math career for one in programming, who said to him "automatic computers were here to stay, that we were just at the beginning and could not [he, Dijkstra] be one of the persons called to make programming a respectable discipline in the years to come?"[3]

Dijkstra rose to the challenge and proceeded to commit himself to doing exactly that.

Lest the reader think that I am overstating the case of how little people thought of programming in 1957, allow me to provide the following anecdote[4]: when Dijkstra married Maria Debets, he was required to state his profession. His declaration that he was a programmer was not accepted by the authorities because there was no such profession at that time in The Netherlands.

Dijkstra, along with other academics such as Niklaus Wirth focused much of their efforts around ALGOL (remember that Algorithmic language I mentioned before?) as the flag

---

[3] Dijkstra, Edsger W. "The Humble Programmer". *Communications Of The ACM*, vol 15, no. 10, 1972, pp. 859-866. *Association For Computing Machinery (ACM)*, doi:10.1145/355604.361591.

[4] E. W. Dijkstra Archive. & James, Mike (1 May 2013). *"Edsger Dijkstra - The Poetry of Programming"*. i-programmer.info. Retrieved 12 August 2015.

bearer for what they called "structured pro-gramming". Does that mean all programming in assembly, FORTRAN and COBOL was unstructured? In a way, yes, and I will explain further below.

For the first twenty years of programming history, most programmers in the field, the ones writing the programs that got used in real life, were self-taught. There were no schools for programmers, no formal practices, no body of knowledge, no discipline to speak of. Pro-grammers either learned from a mentor or pur-sued their own individual instincts and intui-tions.

A truly delightful tale illustrating this is *The Story of Mel,* posted to Usenet[5] by Ed Nather in 1983. Mel was a *bare metal* program-mer. In fact, the jargon file entry for "bare metal" refers to this very story.

Don't worry if you do not understand every word or technical detail in the story be-low, you'll still enjoy it, and I believe you will get the gist. It is a good-humored tongue-in-cheek response to a somewhat self-serious

---

[5] **"Usenet** is a worldwide distributed discussion system" *https://en.wik-ipedia.org/wiki/Usenet*

letter to the editor of *Datamation* magazine that recycled the *Real Men Don't Eat Quiche* trope of the 1980s and was entitled *Real Programmers Don't Use PASCAL*[6] in which the author claims that FORTRAN is the only language a "real programmer" would use. Pascal is a very structured language, perhaps the most structured of them all. I will explain about this right after the story.

The story of Mel

A recent article devoted to the *macho* side of programming made the bald and unvarnished statement:

Real Programmers write in Fortran.

Maybe they do now, in this decadent era of Lite beer, hand calculators and "user-friendly" software but back in the Good Old Days, when the term "software" sounded funny and Real Computers were made out of drums and vacuum tubes, Real Programmers wrote in machine code. Not Fortran. Not RATFOR. Not, even, assembly language. Machine Code. Raw, unadorned, inscrutable hexadecimal numbers. Directly.

Lest a whole new generation of programmers grow up in ignorance of this glorious past, I feel duty-bound to describe, as best I can through the generation gap, how a Real

---

[6] *Post, Ed (July 1983). "Real Programmers Don't Use Pascal". Datamation. Archived from the original on 2012-02-02. "... Real Programmers use FORTRAN. Quiche Eaters use PASCAL ..."*

Programmer wrote code. I'll call him Mel, because that was his name.

I first met Mel when I went to work for Royal McBee Computer Corp., a now-defunct subsidiary of the typewriter company. The firm manufactured the LGP-30, a small, cheap (by the standards of the day) drum-memory computer, and had just started to manufacture the RPC-4000, a much-improved, bigger, better, faster -- drum-memory computer. Cores cost too much, and weren't here to stay, anyway. (That's why you haven't heard of the company, or the computer.)

I had been hired to write a Fortran compiler for this new marvel and Mel was my guide to its wonders. Mel didn't approve of compilers.

"If a program can't rewrite its own code," he asked, "what good is it?"

Mel had written, in hexadecimal, the most popular computer program the company owned. It ran on the LGP-30 and played blackjack with potential customers at computer shows. Its effect was always dramatic. The LGP-30 booth was packed at every show, and the IBM salesmen stood around talking to each other. Whether or not this actually sold computers was a question we never discussed.

Mel's job was to re-write the blackjack program for the RPC-4000. (Port? What does that mean?) The new computer had a one-plus-one addressing scheme, in which each machine instruction, in addition to the operation code and the address of the needed operand, had a second address that indicated where, on the revolving drum, the next instruction was located. In modern parlance, every single instruction was followed by a GO TO! Put *that* in Pascal's pipe and smoke it.

Mel loved the RPC-4000 because he could optimize his code: that is, locate instructions on the drum so that just as one finished its job, the next would be just arriving at the "read head" and available for immediate execution. There was a program to do that job, an "optimizing assembler", but Mel refused to use it.

"You never know where it's going to put things", he explained, "so you'd have to use separate constants".

It was a long time before I understood that remark. Since Mel knew the numerical value of every operation code, and assigned his own drum addresses, every instruction he wrote could also be considered a numerical constant. He could pick up an earlier "add" instruction, say, and multiply by it, if it had the right numeric value. His code was not easy for someone else to modify.

I compared Mel's hand-optimized programs with the same code massaged by the optimizing assembler program, and Mel's always ran faster. That was because the "top-down" method of program design hadn't been invented yet, and Mel wouldn't have used it anyway. He wrote the innermost parts of his program loops first, so they would get first choice of the optimum address locations on the drum. The optimizing assembler wasn't smart enough to do it that way.

Mel never wrote time-delay loops, either, even when the balky Flexowriter required a delay between output characters to work right. He just located instructions on the drum so each successive one was just *past* the read head when it was needed; the drum had to execute another complete revolution to find the next instruction. He coined an unforgettable term for this procedure. Although "optimum" is an absolute term, like "unique", it became common verbal practice to make it relative: "not quite optimum" or "less optimum" or "not very optimum". Mel called the maximum time-delay locations the "most pessimum".

After he finished the blackjack program and got it to run, ("Even the initializer is optimized", he said proudly) he got a Change Request from the sales department. The program used an elegant (optimized) random number generator to shuffle the "cards" and deal from the "deck", and some of the salesmen felt it was too fair, since sometimes the customers lost. They wanted Mel to modify the program so, at the setting of a sense switch on the console, they could change the odds and let the customer win.

Mel balked. He felt this was patently dishonest, which it was, and that it impinged on his personal integrity as a programmer, which it did, so he refused to do it. The Head Salesman talked to Mel, as did the Big Boss and, at the boss's urging, a few Fellow Programmers. Mel finally gave in and wrote the code, but he got the test backwards, and, when the sense switch was turned on, the program would cheat, winning every time. Mel was delighted with this, claiming his subconscious was uncontrollably ethical, and adamantly refused to fix it.

After Mel had left the company for greener pa$ture$, the Big Boss asked me to look at the code and see if I could find the test and reverse it. Somewhat reluctantly, I agreed to look. Tracking Mel's code was a real adventure.

I have often felt that programming is an art form, whose real value can only be appreciated by another versed in the same arcane art; there are lovely gems and brilliant coups hidden from human view and admiration, sometimes forever, by the very nature of the process. You can learn a lot about an individual just by reading through his code, even in hexadecimal. Mel was, I think, an unsung genius.

Perhaps my greatest shock came when I found an innocent loop that had no test in it. No test. *None*. Common sense said it had to be a closed loop, where the program would circle, forever, endlessly. Program control passed right through it, however, and safely out the other side. It took me two weeks to figure it out.

The RPC-4000 computer had a really modern facility called an index register. It allowed the programmer to write a program loop that used an indexed instruction inside; each time through, the number in the index register was added to the address of that instruction, so it would refer to the next datum in a series. He had only to increment the index register each time through. Mel never used it.

Instead, he would pull the instruction into a machine register, add one to its address, and store it back. He would then execute the modified instruction right from the register. The loop was written so this additional execution time was taken into account -- just as this instruction finished, the next one was right under the drum's read head, ready to go. But the loop had no test in it.

The vital clue came when I noticed the index register bit, the bit that lay between the address and the operation code in the instruction word, was turned on-- yet Mel never used the index register, leaving it zero all the time. When the light went on it nearly blinded me.

He had located the data he was working on near the top of memory -- the largest locations the instructions could address -- so, after the last datum was handled, incrementing the instruction address would make it overflow. The carry would add one to the operation code, changing it to the next one in the instruction set: a jump instruction. Sure enough, the next program instruction was in address location zero, and the program went happily on its way.

I haven't kept in touch with Mel, so I don't know if he ever gave in to the flood of change that has washed over programming techniques since those long-gone days. I like to think he didn't. In any event, I was impressed enough that I quit looking for the offending test, telling the Big Boss I couldn't find it. He didn't seem surprised.

When I left the company, the blackjack program would still cheat if you turned on the right sense switch, and I think that's how it should be. I didn't feel comfortable hacking up the code of a Real Programmer.

LIBRASCOPE'S MURAL ROOM became a study hall for neophyte LPG-30 programmers the week of July 16. Students participating in this first training school for LPG-30 customers included (seated l. to r.) Bill Hopper, Mary Cornell and Chuck Rue, Convair-Pomona; John Corkhill, Convair-San Diego; R. J. Bibbins, Link Aviation; K. A. Hurst, D. D. Parkhurst, C. S. Kikushima and Ides J. Romero, Convair-San Diego; George Kendrick, Convair-Pomona; Chuck Ray, Caltech; and William Clayton, National Security Agency. Standing (l. to r.) are Fred Flannell, class instructor and assistant sales manager of Royal-McBee; and Royal-McBee Applications Engineers Bud Hazlett, Jack Behr and Mel Kaye.   (Photo by Duggan)

Mel Kaye, standing, far right.

As the story so wonderfully illustrates, the first few generations of programmers were quite accustomed to doing as they wished, using idiosyncratic methods and highly personal styles of programming. And there was sometimes resentment among them towards the academics and their efforts to promote structured programming.

For the benefit of readers who are not programmers, the concept of structured programming was closely tied to programming languages, so one speaks of a "structured programming language" or sometimes simply a "structured language". In an unstructured language, the format of the code will not give us any clues about the *flow of control* (the order in which statements or instructions are executed). Here is what that looks like written in *pseudo code* (a description of a program that is not written in any specific computer language):

```
1    START PROGRAM
2    GET list_of_names from user
3    COUNT = number of items in list_of_names
4    READ first item from list_of_names
5    DO thing a
6    DO thing b
7    IF result of thing b is TRUE GOTO line 11
8    DO thing c
9    DO thing d
10   END IF
```

```
11    DELETE first item from list_of_names

12    SUBTRACT 1 from COUNT

13    IF COUNT = 0

14    EXIT

15    END IF

16    GOTO LINE 4

17    END IF

18    END PROGRAM
```

This code will loop as long as there are names in the list to process, and it will jump over lines 8 & 9 if the result of line 7 "evaluates" as TRUE. Just by glancing at it there is nothing in the structure of this code to tell you that. You have to read it line by line to know. And even then, there is no clue to tell you that lines 8 & 9 are *special* cases and that the "result of thing b" is usually TRUE.

A "structured language" would be one that did not provide a GOTO instruction (lines 7 & 16 above) and instead provided higher level concepts such as WHILE and FUNCTION, as in the example below:

```
START PROGRAM

GET list_of_names from user


WHILE list_of_names is not empty

    READ first item from list_of_names

    DO thing a

    DO thing b
```

```
    IF result of thing b is TRUE
        DO somethingSpecial
    END IF
    DELETE first item from list_of_names
END WHILE


FUNCTION somethingSpecial
    DO thing c
    DO thing d
END FUNCTION
END PROGRAM
```

These two examples do the same thing(s); however, proponents of structured programming argue the second one is more readable, less error prone, and easier/faster to write, therefore enhancing productivity. Readability in particular, matters because as it happens, programmers spend quite a bit more time reading already written code then they do writing new code[7].

During the sixties, Dijkstra published seven papers. In a 1996 poll of over a thousand professors of computer science, four of Dijkstra's papers were selected as being among the thirty-eight most influential papers on computer science ever written. But by far his most

---

[7] Martin, Robert C., and Lei Han. Clean code. Publishing House of Electronics Industry, 2012

famous contribution was a short five-page letter in defense of structured programming sent in 1968 to the editor of the *Journal of The Association for Computing Machinery*, the leading publication in computer science at the time. Dijkstra sent the letter with the undramatic title: *A Case Against the Goto Statement*, but editor Niklaus Wirth (who created Pascal in 1970) somewhat mischievously changed the title, using a popular journalistic cliché of the times, to *Go To Statement Considered Harmful*.

This letter to the editor triggered at least two decades of debate and remains (probably) the most recognizable (yet least read) computer science article of all time. One does not have to look far to find contemporary citations and discussion. The publication was significant in many ways, not least of which was that it triggered one of the earliest (perhaps the first) of the *Holy Wars*[8] or the *Religious Wars* of which *Real Programmers Don't USE PASCAL* and *The Story of Mel* are just small examples. From 1970 onwards advances in programming would be punctuated by rabid advocacy and totalitarian claims of supremacy for competing conceptual models.

---

[8] http://www.catb.org/jargon/html/H/holy-wars.html

Programming, perhaps more so than any other applied science, inspires a fanatical quest for perfection and purity. Fred Brooks suggests that it might be due to the fact that *"The programmer, like the poet, works only slightly removed from pure thought-stuff. He builds his castles in the air, from air, creating by exertion of the imagination. Few media of creation are so flexible, so easy to polish and rework, so readily capable of realizing grand conceptual structures".*[9]

An article in the Business Insider in 2015[10] offers this somewhat less romantic explanation of "Why coders get into 'religious wars' over programming languages", saying, "… every programming language represents a philosophy as much as it does a product".

Since *Go To Statement Considered Harmful* was first published there has been no lack of reasons to start a war. Prior to its publication only 200 languages had been created, but in the time since, a few thousand more came into being.

---

[9] Brooks, Frederick P. *The Mythical Man-Month And Other Essays On Software Engineering*. Chapel Hill, Dept. Of Computer Science, University Of North Carolina At Chapel Hill, 1974, p.21

[10] http://www.businessinsider.com/why-coders-get-into-religious-wars-over-programming-languages-2015-6

There are many important languages that I will not write about in this book. For example, I love the Python and Ruby languages, but they do not play a significant role in corporate IT and project failure. You will instead find Python being used by researchers for data mining and artificial intelligence. Also, both Python and Ruby are often found in Internet companies like Google, Dropbox, or Uber and in startup companies galore. As I say at the beginning, I am writing about IT project failure in government and traditional enterprise.

Illumination and marginalia

I think of the first two decades after 1949 as the dark ages of programming. Historical documentation abounds for the computers themselves, as I wrote earlier, hardware engineering was highly respected and recognized. The profession of electrical engineering was well organized, well documented, and acknowledged as being very significant. Yet the *programmers* labored in obscurity.

The typical programmer was self-taught and highly internally motivated. Apart from a small number of young prodigies, a programmer was more likely than not already highly educated, often with a master's degree or a PhD (which was how come they came to be anywhere near a computer to begin with). They tended to be a *very* smart bunch.

There were no schools or courses for programmers. And with computers costing millions of dollars there were no casual programmers. They were some of the brightest lights of humanity simply by virtue of how difficult it was to become a programmer at that time.

For every Dijkstra or Knuth or Wirth that we know about, there were a thousand Mels, creating works of pure genius, of elegance and rare beauty, that were to be forever lost as the magnetic tapes and punch cards that preserved the deepest thoughts of this hidden generation became obsolete and were binned, unceremoniously and out of sight.

"The trouble with programmers is that you can never tell what a programmer is doing until it's too late."

~ Seymour Cray
Inventor of the Cray supercomputer

Chapter Three
The winds of change: 1970-1980

If the previous two decades were the dark ages, the 1970's were the Renaissance; a bridge between the classical era of computing and the modern era of programming. It was a time of great change for Western society in general and the world of programming was no exception. Programming was on the verge of becoming the activity we know today; it was increasingly possible to write code without an intimate knowledge of the computer hardware. CRT based VDTs first introduced with IBM's System 360 and originally costing as much again as the computer itself, became affordable and common. New programming languages changed the way people worked, and by the end of the decade, personal computers became available at reasonable prices.

The 1970's are also when my narrative starts to become personal. Although I myself did not start to program until the eighties, the programmer culture and history of the seventies was still a very real and contemporary presence for me as I learned the craft. The people I write about, most of whom were heroes to me, were in the prime of their careers when I was just starting mine, and I have personally used most of the systems and languages that I will write about from this point on.

One system that was tremendously important was Unix™. It was created by a team of five programmers at AT&T Bell Laboratories and was portable from one hardware platform to another. Its distribution included the source code for the OS itself. For this reason, Unix™ was "ported" to many different hardware platforms. It was the beginning of operating systems that were independent of specific hardware platforms. It would be difficult to overstate the influence that Unix™ has had on computing in general, but more specifically on the craft[1] of programming.

From the perspective of personal computers (my own perspective), which initially ran crude little operating systems like MS-DOS and CP/M, Unix™ had the aura of "the big leagues"; rich in features, impressively flexible, at times arcane and inscrutable, at others powerful and simple. When I started working in Unix™ I felt I had arrived. In my own eyes, and that of my boss, I was elite. When GE

---

[1] Programming is both an art, as Knuth would have it, and a craft. The two are not mutually exclusive. When talking about creativity it is art. When talking about rigor and mastery it is a craft

Information Services was asked by GM's Electronic Data Systems to setup a Unix™ server farm to control the computerized painting of Camaro automobiles at their Sainte-Thérèse plant, I was the one they sent. I knew Unix™! However, from the perspective of the real big leagues — operating systems for mainframes and minicomputers — nothing could be further from reality.

Unix™ was developed by a team working on a "real" operating system: Multics. In those days "real" operating systems (used by "real" programmers) ran on huge, powerful, extremely expensive computers. One of their jobs was to manage this expensive resource as carefully as possible. Therefore, significant portions of their code were dedicated to complicated user management, with accounts that had quotas or allocations of computer time, and code to remove time from the account as program "jobs" were run. They managed the separation between jobs, the "time-slicing" that optimized the use of the CPU, the communications protocols to terminals and disks and printers, and a long list of other things besides.

The name Unix was a typical programmer's joke, a play on words. Designed as a playground for developers, it intentionally lacked all the complicated controls of Multics, and so it was *Un*-Multics, as well it was *Uni*-user because it lacked what were considered standard *multi*-user features. But at the same time, the OS itself was a very serious endeavor. It was meant to be a productive platform for programmers to develop software and it had a single unifying philosophy: "the idea that the power of a system comes more from the relationships among programs than from the programs themselves".[2] It had architectural coherence: terminals, printers, and even disks and network adaptors were all treated the same way through a single simple communications model.

And it was programmable.

When one purchased Unix™ from AT&T (for the princely sum of twenty-thousand dollars) it came with the source code. The implications of that were staggering for the time. Up until this time, operating systems were almost exclusively created by the computer hardware manufacturers for a specific computer or series of computers and were jealously guarded trade secrets. It was not only impossible - it was unthinkable - to modify the OS in any way. By the unorthodox inclusion of the source code,

---

[2] Kernighan, Brian W, and Rob Pike. *The UNIX Programming Environment*. Englewood Cliffs, N.J., Prentice-Hall, 1984.

AT&T made it possible for any licensee to do two things that were completely novel: they could modify it, and they could compile it and run it on any computer that had a C compiler (which very quickly became quite a few), and *that* meant that a programmer could replace the original operating system that came with the computer!

Not that AT&T was completely free from the closely guarded trade secret mentality. Every time I have written Unix above, I included a trademark symbol next to it. This is an in-joke for any reader who happened to have been a programmer in the 70's and 80's. AT&T was infamous for its fanatical pursuit of trademark infringement. Usenet lore had it that even a casual mention of Unix without the ™ would bring down a storm of corporate legal aggression so fearsome that it could take years off of one's life. As such, many of us carefully, and very ironically, inserted (tm) after every mention of the name. I hope I gave a smile to at least one or two readers.

So how did Unix help improve productivity in programming? Because of its philosophy of placing a premium on interactions between programs, Unix dictated a standard simple protocol by which programs would exchange data with other programs and with the computer and all its peripherals: text.

This sounds deceptively trivial. It is anything but. Anyone with even passing technical familiarity with Unix has heard the phrase: "in Unix, everything is a file". What this means in practical terms is that a program does nothing differently *at all* to send the sentence "Hello World" to a printer, to the screen, to another program, or to a file on disk for storage because all of these things appear to the program as a file on disk. In fact, in traditional Unix usage, the program would not do any of these things itself. The *user* (who is also a programmer) would. The user would type the command **HelloWorldProgram > lpt1** to direct the "standard output" (called **stdout**) of the Hello World program to Line Printer 1 or **HelloWorldProgram | WordCount** to *pipe* the output of Hello World to a program that would count how many words it received on its "standard input". By standardizing the way programs exchanged data with anything outside of themselves Unix promoted a way of thinking that was to have a profound effect on the way programs were written. When you use your Facebook account to log into some other website, you are benefiting from the philosophy that Unix pioneered of different programs working together seamlessly. When your phone opens the map program to give you directions, or opens the email program to send an email, it is because Unix taught programmers that "the power of a system comes more from the relationships among programs than from the programs themselves".

Because of this, Unix programs are often small, doing one thing only, such as **tail**, which reads in a file (remember: *everything* is a file) and sends the last 10 lines to its standard output, and it is normal for programs to be written with other programs in mind. For example, the Unix program **man**, which shows the user manual entries for various programs. The author of man did not bother to write code to break up long manual pages into readable chunks, because according to the philosophy of Unix, the output of **man** should be *piped* to another program such as either **less** or **more**, which are "paging" programs that break long files (remember: *everything* is a file) into pages the size of the screen, allowing the user to "turn" the pages by pressing the space bar.

Because of this philosophy, the programmer of **man** was able to leverage the previous work done by the programmer of **less** (or **more**). As you might imagine, this new approach to writing programs had a dramatic effect on productivity.

Smaller programs are easier to write, have fewer bugs, are easier to debug when needed, and are easier to maintain. If you clean your kitchen a little bit every day, it is a lot easier than trying one big cleanup every month. Programming is exactly like that, so writing smaller programs, that rely upon other previously written (and already tested and debugged) programs, is more productive than writing big "kitchen sink" programs. Or as I call them: "world domination programs".

This is a *very* important idea. I will come back to it towards the end of the book, so please make a mental note of the Unix philosophy that the best way to approach programming is by writing small program components within a powerful unifying framework, and then linking them together.

There was one more thing…

In 1972 the Unix team created a language to help them write their operating system. The language was called C. It is arguably the most influential programming language ever created. I could also argue that it set productivity back by a couple of decades.

Productivity

The word productivity comes with a lot of baggage. For many years, programmer productivity was measured in lines of code per day/week/month. There are several flaws in this method.

Let's take a small game program called **life** and have two programmers of different skill levels write it in two languages: C and assembly. In C this is a 57-line program. The assembly language version is 97 lines. Let's say that the C programmer takes sixty seconds per line (this is actually very fast) and the assembly programmer writes code even faster than the C programmer at the rate of one line every 40 seconds. It will take 65 minutes to create the assembly language version versus 57 minutes for the C version, so it took 15% more time, even though the assembly programmer writes 33% more lines of code per day.

Can we say that the assembly language programmer was more productive? If we measure by lines of code a day, she definitely was. If we measure by time spent to achieve results, no. Things get even less clear when you consider that the two programmers may be making different salaries because a programmer might also be paid less and therefore *cost* less "per line".

Can we at least compare two programmers making the same salary, working in the same language? Let us consider this case: two programmers write the game of `life` in C. Captain Slow as we shall call him takes an entire day to write 97 lines of highly optimized code that takes 100 kilobytes of disk and loads in less than a second. Captain Showboat takes the same day, manages to find a way to use 970 lines of code where 97 would do just fine, to write a program that takes up one megabyte of disk and takes 10 seconds to load.

Now tell me: who is the more productive programmer?

More code does not automatically make a program better. Do we really want to incentivize people to write more lines than necessary? Bill Gates famously denigrated measuring productivity by lines of code by calling it a race "to build the world's heaviest airplane".[3]

Another favorite unit of measure is "function points", a conceptual unit that is supposed

---

[3] "The Physicist". *Wired*, 1995, https://www.wired.com/1995/09/myhrvold/.

to represent a discrete functionality for the end user. For example, the ability to login would be one function point (FP). The ability to change your profile photo would be another. In the real world, almost nobody counts the function points or has the ability to track how much programmer time was spent on a given FP. Therefore, almost everybody who measures productivity in FP/day "cheats" by using industry standard *conversion factors* that say: language x typically uses y lines of code per FP. Then you take the lines of code and divide by the conversion factor, which gives you an estimated number of function points. Obviously, this is no better than counting lines of code. There are two or three other methods of measuring programmer productivity, none of them any better.

Therefore, when I write about productivity in software development, I am appealing to common sense, not metrics. I consider an improvement in productivity to be anything that helps get the software *product* successfully completed faster or better without costing more.

Of novices and masters

My reason for saying that C could possibly have set productivity back by a few decades is deeply connected to the central thesis of this book that modern programming is *artisanal* and cannot succeed without master programmers. My absolute favorite programming joke (from the *Jargon File*, of course) is written in the style of a *koan*, a riddle intended to help a Zen monk achieve enlightenment.

> **A novice was trying to fix a broken Lisp machine by turning the power off and on.**
>
> **Knight, seeing what the student was doing, spoke sternly: "You cannot fix a machine by just power-cycling it with no understanding of what is going wrong".**
>
> **Knight turned the machine off and on.**
>
> **The machine worked.**

Tom Knight, one of the Lisp[4] machine's principal designers, *knew what he was doing* when he power-cycled the machine, which is why it worked for him and not for the novice, who had no understanding of what was going wrong.

C is like that; it is almost assembly language. It is powerful, and it is dangerous. It is magic. In the hands of a master programmer, the proper incantations in C can be used to write an operating system, another language, or operate devices that our very lives depend

---

[4] You will probably remember I mentioned LISP in Chapter One, an influential computer language in use since the late 1950s.

upon such as the anti-lock brakes on your car. In the hands of people not quite sure of what they are doing, the magic spell could destroy a piece of hardware, wipe out data, or leave a subtle bug that will not be discovered for a long time and will be almost impossible to track down once the undesired side effects are noticed.

C brought programming back to the days of Mel, whose brilliant trickery would have been impossible in FORTRAN, COBOL, or ALGOL. It would also be impossible in the other new languages becoming available at the time; BASIC, Pascal, Forth, and Smalltalk. Yet in C you have only to point to a memory address and away you go. Just like Mel.

And here's the thing:

If every programmer were as good as Mel, this kind of programming would be just lovely. We would all be using optimized code that ran super-fast and didn't make mistakes. But the harsh reality is that *not every programmer is that good*. And it was at the same time as C was released, that things were going to get a lot worse in that respect.

Barbarians at the gate

Up until now, because of the cost of computers, there were mostly two kinds of programmers: a) professionals working for government or large corporations, and b) academics, often postgraduates, using programming for research. Both kinds were almost exclusively self-taught, very smart, and almost *always* had a real affinity or talent for coding.

But now, in the seventies, two important things changed. First, academic institutions were creating curricula specifically for programming, creating new "teaching languages", and most importantly, undergraduates (and the occasional lucky high schooler) were being given time-sharing accounts specifically for the purpose of learning how to program.

The second thing that changed was the advent of personal computers, first as kits assembled at home, then later as attractively packaged consumer goods that sold for the same price as an old used car. It was going to get a lot easier for those who did have an affinity to teach themselves. The first mass produced computer kit, the Altair 8800, shipped 5,000 units in 1975, its first year of production. In three years (1977-1979) the two top personal computers - the Tandy TRS-80[5] and the Apple II - sold more than 150,000 units. Between 1975 and 1980, the number of computers in the world doubled. It had just become a heck of a lot easier to get anywhere near a computer to begin with.

The BASIC language was usually the only software that was included, and hundreds of thousands of new programmers were either being taught or were teaching themselves, and they would soon be unleashed into the world, a world that was hungry for computer programs. They would soon dramatically swell the ranks of programmers.

It was no longer so very hard to become a programmer, and programming was becoming known as a promising *career* that one could *train* for. Once the object of passion and care, programming was on its way to becoming a lucrative career that would attract all sorts of people who, with no particular passion or affinity, were only in it for the money.

---

[5] My little brother was one of those people. I, a musician, was interested in his TRS-80 for almost ten minutes. If you had told either one of us that day that he would become a professional artist, and I would be a computer geek, we both would have thought you were completely crazy.

Of myth and man

The last thing from the seventies that I want to tell you about is the publication in 1975 of *The Mythical Man-Month*. This oft-quoted book by a former IBM manager named Frederick P. Brooks Jr. describes the lessons he learned ten years earlier while managing one of the biggest software development projects to that date, the System/360 operating system.

It is astonishing to me that in re-reading it now, I cannot find a single analysis or observation that is not as pertinent and trenchant today as it was over forty years ago when this book of essays first came out. *The Mythical Man-Month* was a seminal work. It is impossible to overstate its significance and the impact and influence it has had on the entire computing industry. Although I think no one at the time recognized it, it was the first *comprehensive* software development lifecycle (SDLC) methodology. Not only did it describe the challenges faced by systems programming, it prescribed (in over 150 pages):

- the phases of SDLC
- the allocation of time for each cycle
- how to estimate
- how to staff
- how to structure the organization

- how to manage the design of the program
- how to plan iteration
- documentation and governance
- communications protocols
- how to measure productivity
- some special concerns around code design
- deliverables and artifacts
- tools and frameworks
- how to debug and plan releases
- how to manage the process

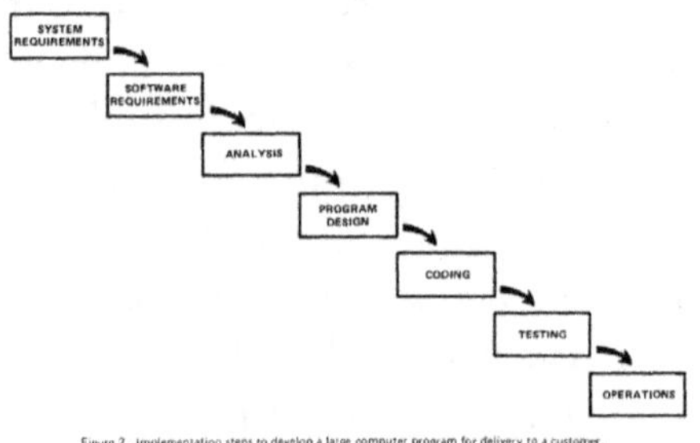

Figure 2. Implementation steps to develop a large computer program for delivery to a customer.

It is true that the illustration of a step by step path in *Figure 2* above had appeared in W.W. Royce's 1970 paper *Managing the Development of Large Software Systems* but contrary to what many people believe, Royce was not advocating its use. In fact, he issued warnings about using it. He was simply describing common practice of the time and some of the problems associated with it. And just as Brooks did five years later, he made some proposals on how to mitigate the issues.

However, Royce's recommendations filled ten pages, compared to the 150 pages of detailed prescriptions that are in *The Mythical Man-Month*. Royce's paper is not so much a methodology as a call to action. That is why I credit Brooks with the first written methodology.

I'll talk more about methodologies a few chapters from now, but not just yet. There are still a few stories to tell about programming languages in the eighties.

"Do NOT simply read the instructions in here without understanding what they do."

The configuration file that comes bundled with the Apache webserver

Chapter Four
Objectively speaking: 1980 - 1990

Bigger than a breadbox

In the eighties, a new kind of computer started to become common, the *workstation[1]*. At first, the Xerox Corporation's Palo Alto Research Center created a workstation called the Alto but it was never commercialized. The main companies selling workstations were Sun, Apollo, and Silicon Graphics (SGI), and then later on, Hewlett-Packard and IBM. At the very end of the decade a workstation called the NeXT[2] was created by Steve Jobs.

Workstations were powerful professional versions of personal computers that cost as much as a *new* car (compared to consumer personal computers that were the cost of a *used* car). They were designed to be used for engineering tasks such as digital animation (the specialty of SGI), newspaper layout (Apollo's stronghold), or running computing centers and

---

[1] If a train station is where the train stops, what's a workstation? *(typical programmer humor)*

[2] Believe it or not: the iPhone is directly descended from the NeXT.

CAD or Computer-aided design (Sun). The NeXT workstation would be the world's first web server. A lot of the programs written for these new computers were written in new languages.

For the first time since COBOL, languages were going to have a greater effect on productivity than hardware or OS. Of the many languages that emerged during this decade (at least 65 of them), there were three new languages developed for these workstations that left a lasting impact on programming for *all* computers.

Smalltalk because it profoundly influenced almost every language that came after it.

C++ because it is so ubiquitous it has to be mentioned even though I maintain it did not change the craft of programming as much as Smalltalk or Objective-C did.

And finally, Objective-C because it is a story of how class libraries that come packaged with a language can dramatically improve productivity and be so flexible that they can power hundreds of generations of devices over decades.

Good things come in Smalltalk packages

Smalltalk was actually first written in 1972 but was kept within the Xerox Palo Alto Research Center (PARC) for eight years. In 1980, a new version was released and distributed to four companies for peer review and implementation: Tektronix, Hewlett-Packard, Digital Equipment Corp, and Apple. I estimate that Smalltalk ranks equal to C in terms of importance and impact upon computers and programming productivity.

One of the many ways in which it was influential was that it came with a development environment. Integrated Development Environments (IDEs) are commonplace today, but prior to Smalltalk most programmers wrote code with a text editor (something that is making a bit of a comeback in recent years). Small Talk came with a special tool that not only organized the code in a *repository*, but also helped you see which bits of code were connected to which other bits, and it allowed for the examination of the code *as it ran*. Before this, programmers would have to embed debugging messages (sent to themselves while the program was running) so they could see how far the program executed before crashing. They had to use hardware features to step through code one instruction at a time and would take snapshots of memory called core dumps.

Smalltalk was the first language to include a development environment that supported live examination of the program as it ran, which meant that developers could instantly see all the implications of any code they wrote. Want to know if an index starts at zero or if it starts at one? Just try it out – "ask the compiler". It is faster than looking it up. Smalltalk was the most interactive programming language ever to appear.

Many modern languages such as Java would be completely unusable without some of the IDE concepts that Smalltalk pioneered.

Smalltalk also was the first general-purpose Object-Oriented Programming (OOP) language. Almost every language currently used today uses objects. Smalltalk showed us how.

Objects were seen as a way to get control of code reuse. Since the earliest days of programming, coders would reuse favorite bits of code to implement routines and functions that were common to most programs. As ever, this code reuse was highly idiosyncratic, varying in every way from one programmer to another.

As well, bug fixes and enhancements made to one copy were not available to all the other programs in which the code was copied.

The way objects work is that there is a "class library". The classes are templates or blueprints for objects and the main code of the program will use them to "instantiate" or build objects. Since the code of the program is separate from the class library, a class can be updated with a bug fix. Thus, any program that uses that library can be recompiled and the bug fix will be automatically incorporated without rewriting any of the program code. At least in theory.

Almost all popular languages today use this obvious improvement over cutting and pasting scraps of code from a notebook.

Objects are an abstraction layer, which is what you call it when underlying complexity is hidden behind a model. A good example of that is television channels. Channels are abstractions of radio frequencies. When you tune a television to "channel 2" what you are actually doing is adjusting the television's circuitry so that it picks up the radio frequencies between 54 and 60 megahertz and ignores all other radio signals.

FORTRAN and other languages are abstractions of assembly code, and assembly code is an abstraction of machine code. Object oriented languages added a 3rd level of abstraction.

Modern software uses many levels of abstraction. When you interact with a web page you are dealing with at least a dozen layers of abstraction. The "button" you click on is really a region of the screen which is caught by the operating system, passed to the web browser, which compares it to a pixel map in memory which was rendered from a "Document Object Model" which was constructed by interpreting HTML (and CSS and JavaScript), which calls HTTP functions that in turn call TCP/IP protocols, which deliver messages to and responses from an "Application Programming Interface" which is usually built from one or more "frameworks" which are abstractions of the language they are written in, which are themselves abstractions of assembly language which is an abstraction of machine code.

And this is highly simplified. The reality is that there are actually *many more* layers involved.

However, in the eighties, programmers were still working pretty "close to the metal".

There were only the operating system abstraction and the language abstraction(s). And good programmers were aware of what was below. Good programmers, even if they did not write in assembly code, knew how to read it, and knew how their code translated to assembly – at least in areas critical for performance.

Apple Computer was strongly influenced by the work being done at Xerox PARC. Apple had made a deal with Xerox, letting them buy 100,000 shares of stock for $1M (worth $22M one year later, and worth $6.7B today) in exchange for two one day demonstrations of the technology at PARC in 1979 and the right to use what they saw. Xerox did okay.

Unlike the Xerox management, Apple management was intent upon putting these ideas into the hands of customers. Naturally some of the best minds at Xerox eventually came to work for Apple, and ideas came with them.

Although Apple had access to Smalltalk, it used Pascal as its official development language, and so it ended up extending the Pascal language to include objects. This was Object Pascal. It then created an object library or framework called MacApp which was intended to create major productivity gains for developers. It missed the mark because it had too many levels of inheritance and was too complex. Instead of simplifying development it made it more complex in many ways. Which is why you probably have never heard of it.

C goes to class

Before Smalltalk, there existed another language that used objects. It was called Simula. It was not a general-purpose language. It was specifically designed to run simulations in research settings. Bjarne Stroustrup, a Danish computer scientist, got to know it while working on his Ph.D. thesis. Later, when he was working for AT&T Bell Labs, he was given the problem of updating Unix for distributed computing.

Distributed computing is exactly what it sounds like. A computer program that runs on more than one computer. To do this successfully, the program has to be separated into chunks, and because networking between computers is not 100% reliable, those chunks have to be made independent of each other somehow. Objects are a good way to do this, and this is what made Stroustrup think of Simula.

Before OOP, it was common practice to use something called global variables. A global variable is a way to store a piece of information that needs to be used, and possibly changed at different times, by different bits of code that are in different places in the program.

For example, if a large company needs an audit trail to keep track of modifications to **accountBalance**, then I have to have code to do that in each subroutine on every computer that can send modifications to **accountBalance**. Since the subroutines must be synchronized, if I change the way I do it in one subroutine, I have to remember to find all other subroutines and change it there too. If these subroutines were running on different computers, I would need to design some sort of shared memory among physically separate CPUs or computers.

I could create a *global variable* called "**accountBalance**" and initialize it to zero. Then in my program I would have subroutines for deposit and withdrawal, which would add to or subtract from **accountBalance**. There are a number of problems with this tactic that mostly center around conflicts that arise from many pieces of code never "knowing" if another piece of code has changed what was stored in that shared piece of memory.

In OOP, I could create a special class called a singleton that can only be used to construct one instance, one object. This would be a self-contained package of code that did everything there was to be done in regard to changing the account balance. It would create its own *private* variable, and it would know how to keep and store a record of changes to it without any potential conflicts, and how to queue requests that arrived at the same time. It would have error checking and validation code. And it would have code to increment and decrement the amount stored. It would then "publish" what are called public methods.

Methods are methods of access. So, my object, which I will call **accountBalanceObject** has an increment method and a decrement method. In most languages "calling" the method would look like this: **accountBalanceObject.increment** and **accountBalanceObject.decrement**. Whenever I call one of these methods from another object (the *Sender*) I pass an amount along with the call (as a *parameter*) and the code inside **accountBalanceObject** will use that amount to perform the appropriate action(s), and then, **accountBalanceObject** will *return* a value. The *return value* will either be some sort of success code (usually the new value), or some sort of error code. The *Sender* will have code that waits for the return value, and will either proceed if there is success, or take corrective action if there is an error. This way the two objects can now be on separate CPUs and still work properly.

Since Stroustrup was familiar with objects from using Simula for his PhD. Thesis, he followed a natural course of action by taking C, which is the language in which Unix was already written in and adding objects to it. Originally called C with Classes, it was shortened to C++ which is Yet Another[3] programmer's joke. "++" is a programmer's shortcut to add one to a number, and C with Classes was adding to C.

Nowadays C is still used extensively. Most "embedded" systems – that is systems in your car, a vending machine, or a cash register, etc. – are implemented in C. Although C is still a universal language supported on almost every platform, C++ is nearly as universal, and because of the conveniences provided by OOP it is more likely to be used for writing an application. Most Adobe apps are written in C++ because it reduces the effort required to release versions on both Windows and Mac. Important parts of Google, as well as the Chrome browser, the Firefox browser and MySQL are written in C++.

---

[3] http://catb.org/jargon/html/Y/Yet-Another.html

If you have a really big application to write and you want a lot of control over how it uses the hardware C++ will give you the power of C with the convenience of objects to make the job easier, but C++ did not really substantially change the way programmers work. Which might be why it was so very popular. Your *average programmer* is not overly fond of big change. They have invested a lot to learn a language, and do not relish starting again at the bottom.

> **"C makes it easy to shoot yourself in the foot; C++ makes it harder, but when you do, it blows away your whole leg."**
>
> ~ Bjarne Stroustrup

How the Web was won.

The last language we will look at in this chapter is Objective-C, created by Brad Cox and Tom Love in the early eighties. Although concerned with the question of cross platform development, they also had another agenda.

Cox had a Big Idea: interchangeable software components, or Software ICs as he called them. We will take a deep look at the general concept of interchangeability in Part Three of this book, but for now let's just focus on

Objective-C without delving into why the word interchangeable is so significant. For the moment, we will simply say that Cox wanted to apply a well-known manufacturing technique to software, and he wanted to prove that it could be done without a major overhaul and wholesale disruption of software development processes existing at the time. He did it by simply extending C without changing it by adding something called a *pre-processor*.

Whereas C++ is a complete language with its own compiler that compiles directly to machine language, Objective-C was designed to first be converted by the pre-processor to standard C, which was then compiled to machine code. And whereas C++ included only standard libraries for basic operations, Objective-C came with an extensive Class Library intended to promote the concepts of Software ICs, and finally, whereas C++ was followed two years later with a simple reference manual describing the language syntax, Objective-C was released concurrently with *Object-Oriented Programming, An Evolutionary Approach* by Cox and Andy Novobilski describing not only the language, but a systematic approach to object-oriented design and development.

The failure of the Object Pascal based MacApp had obviously been a great learning experience for Steve Jobs because when he directed the acquisition and further development of Objective-C into the NextStep object framework for his NeXT workstation, he and his team hit a home run. NextStep is a robust and very useable framework that is still used extensively today for Macs, iPhones and iPads. It's a tremendous productivity enhancer because it gives developers simple coherent access to complex preprogrammed capabilities... like the channel changer on your TV.

As I mentioned earlier, the World Wide Web was created using the NextStep framework in Objective-C on the NeXT computer. Sir Tim Berners-Lee invented the web as a means of sharing research documents while he was working as a software consultant at the CERN particle physics research facility. He says that because of the simplicity and straightforwardness of the NextStep libraries, creating HTTP and the Web Browser was "was remarkably easy".[4]

Class libraries, of which we will see a lot later on, were the next level of abstraction that would bring about an order of magnitude productivity increase. While one FORTRAN

---

[4] Berners-Lee, Tim. "Steve Jobs And The Actually Usable Computer | W3C Blog". *W3.Org*, 2011, https://www.w3.org/blog/2011/10/steve-jobs/.

instruction might compile to dozens of lines of assembly language, a programmer might use a one-line NextStep *class method call* that contains a few hundred lines of Objective-C that pre-compiles to a few thousand lines of C that compiles to a few tens of thousands of lines of assembly language.

In 1996, Apple acquired NeXT as part of a deal to get Jobs to return to Apple and re-named NeXTstep to Cocoa. Today it powers the apps that run on the iMac, iPhone, iPad, and Apple Watch. In its first year, the iPhone had 65,000 apps, mostly from small independent programmers, because of the ease with which an iPhone app can be developed. This amazing productivity is the result of three things working together in close concert: The Objective-C language which is strongly influenced by Smalltalk; Xcode, Apple's integrated development environment which is a direct descendant of the Smalltalk IDE; and the Cocoa class library. Really the three are inseparable. That is the legacy of Smalltalk.

As he had done so many times before and would do again and again, Steve Jobs had made technology picks that were to have lasting repercussions on the entire computer industry.

"The most important thing in the programming language is the name. A language will not succeed without a good name. I have recently invented a very good name and now I am looking for a suitable language".

~ D. E. Knuth

Chapter Five
J is for Java: 1990-2000

In a class of its own

> While Microsoft does not share all of Oracle's ambitions for Java, we agree that it is a very valuable tool for software developers.
>
> ~ Bill Gates

Sun Microsystems had big plans. They wanted to move from their stronghold of workstations to personal computers. This would increase the market (and the profits) of their recently developed SPARC processor a hundredfold. They joined forces with ON Technology, the company founded by software entrepreneur Mitch Kapor, to create an alternative to Microsoft Windows. Although that joint venture did not pan out, through a series of connected events, Sun ended up in possession of a Smalltalk "clone" written in C.

The Smalltalk clone that Sun inherited included a *virtual machine*, an IDE, and a syntax. It was originally started in C++, but was ultimately delivered using Objective-C. That was the foundation for Java.

In the previous section on Smalltalk I did not mention that it ran using a virtual machine or VM. The idea behind virtual machines is that instead of using a compiler to convert source code to the opcodes of a specific processor, it instead compiled generic opcodes of an imaginary CPU that exists only as a design on paper. Smalltalk was the first programming language designed to *depend exclusively* upon a VM.

The VM is an emulator: it emulates this imaginary CPU by converting its generic opcodes to the real opcodes of the physical CPU it is running on. You can write as many virtual machines as you want, ones that run on IBM CPUs, ones that run on Sun SPARC, ones that run on Intel chips, ones that run on the ARM chips in your phone. Once your program has been converted into the generic opcodes of the VM, it will run on all of these platforms.

The Sun marketers made a really big deal out of this, but Java was not the first language to run on many platforms without a re-write. Long before Java there was ANSI C. And USCD Pascal and Smalltalk. Now we have JavaScript, HTML, and a dozen other languages that very effectively run one source code on any platform. It's really not so special.

Mighty oaks from small talks grow

In 1990, Patrick Naughton, one of the Sun developers, tired of the "directionless mass of dispassionate people" in his group and told the CEO, Scott McNealy, that he was leaving to join Steve Jobs at NeXT. To make a long story short (and it is a long story) McNealy made Naughton an offer he could not refuse: a big raise, some stock and the chance to hand-pick a small team and invent a project from scratch. For that, Naughton recruited his mentor James Gosling, and also Mike Sheridan, a dealmaker.

They named it the Green Project and set up a skunkworks[1], where they decided to make a consumer device; specifically, a device for interactive television that they tried to sell to cable companies. Gosling decided to build upon the Smalltalk clone, which he renamed Oak after a tree that was growing outside the window of his office. He added class libraries similar to the ones included with Objective-C, and he made it highly optimized for performance (consumer electronics do not have a lot of CPU or memory). They worked on this for four

---

[1] A skunkworks (also known as Skunk Works) is a small group of people who work on a project in an unconventional way. The group's purpose is to develop something quickly with minimal management constraints. http://searchcio.techtarget.com/definition/skunkworks

years, failing to achieve commercial success. Then Sun made what was a surprising move in those days: They released the Smalltalk clone on the Internet free for anyone to use. And called it Java.

There is nothing particularly special about Java as a programming language. I know there is no shortage of Java devotees ready to argue endlessly about why Java is Really Great! But it really isn't that great. Not that bad, but not that great either. It did however have a couple of very particular advantages that led to its ubiquity in the market.

Designed as it was for television set-top boxes controlled by a central cable TV company, it was good at two things: operating in a very small memory space and sending programs as objects across a network.

This is why it was possible for the web browser company Netscape to officially adopt it and include a Java virtual machine in the browser. It was actually quite a good decision. It allowed browsers to become delivery mechanisms for small applications that communicated with larger applications on a server. It is what made web-based applications possible, because the first versions of HTML couldn't support a rich enough user interface to allow web applications to compete successfully with desktop applications.

Java also included an extensive and useful class library. And just as the included class libraries of Objective-C made it a more productive language for a broader spectrum of programmers, Java's class libraries did the same thing, and made it much easier to use than C++.

In summary, it was lightweight (at first), solved a real problem (rich web UI), came with good libraries, and was supported by a very large stable company that would be around forever (or so it seemed at the time). And unlike most of the languages available at the time, anyone could use it for free.

As web-based applications became the norm, adoption of Java by IT departments of large organizations increased exponentially. Someone on a web forum I use to read once remarked (without judgment) that Java was the new COBOL "because it's becoming the new de facto standard for enterprise applications". I like that comparison.

Because of its popularity, a lot of effort has been invested in improving Java's original flaws (mostly technical stuff, too boring to get into here). From the perspective of results,

Java does a perfectly good job. But still, I'm not partial to it. Call me petty, but like COBOL, it is too verbose for my liking. Reading java (for me) is like going to a party and getting cornered by *that guy*. The one that just goes on and on about himself, using ten-dollar words when fifty-cent words would do.

Here is "Hello World" in Java:

```java
public class Main {

    public static void main(String[] args) {

        System.out.println("Hello, World!");

    }

}
```

Here it is in Python. I like Python.

```python
print("Hello World")
```

In my very personal opinion, Java occupies a grey area between traditional 3GLs where (like Mel) you really have to understand how the computer works, and 4GLs where you do *not* need to know because someone else has done most of the work for you. Java, much more so than the various C languages, is a language where mediocre programmers can use *cargo cult* programming to get programs up and running that seem to work at first, but that contain ticking time bombs created by the indiscriminate and uninformed copying and pasting of code.

Wikipedia says:

Cargo cult programming is a style of computer programming characterized by the ritual inclusion of code or program structures that serve no real purpose. Cargo cult programming is typically symptomatic of a programmer not understanding either a bug they were attempting to solve or the apparent solution... The term cargo cult programmer may apply when an unskilled or novice computer programmer (or one inexperienced with the problem at hand) copies some program code from one place to another with little or no understanding of how it works or whether it is required in its new position".

It adds:

"The term cargo cult, as an idiom, originally referred to aboriginal religions that grew up in the South Pacific after World War II. The practices of these groups centered on building elaborate mock-ups of airplanes and military landing strips in the hope of summoning the god-like airplanes that had brought marvelous cargo during the war. Use of the term in computer programming probably derives from Richard Feynman's characterization of certain practices as cargo cult science".

Too many Java programmers are just like the novice in the LISP koan, and don't really understand the libraries they are using, nor the code they find on the Internet or copy from some other project that looks like it might do the job.

To be fair[2], the same might be said of programmers working in any of the Smalltalk derivatives that come packaged with extensive class libraries and have a large corpus of public domain software available; which is pretty much every popular language introduced after 1990 with the exception of one called Haskell.

Compared to programming close to the metal, most modern languages enable lazy programming by untalented programmers.

> "Java is sort of the COBOL of the 21st century, I think. It's kind of heavyweight, verbose, and everyone loves to hate it... though not everyone will admit that. But managers kind of like it because it looks like you're getting a lot done. If 100 lines of Java code accomplish a task, then it looks like you've written 100 lines, even though in a different language, it might only take 5 lines."
>
> **Larry Wall, creator of the PERL language**
> https://www.youtube.com/watch?v=LR8fQiskYII

---

[2] To be especially fair, I describe myself as a cargo cult programmer. I cannot write a useful application without copying and pasting someone else's code. On good days I understand it.

No, the other left

Now that I have alienated and angered a few million devout worshipers at the altar of Java, I might as well go on and outrage another few million fanatics who love JavaScript more than life itself.

Netscape undoubtedly played a big part in Java's success, but while adopting Java, it was simultaneously developing a competing language which would one day threaten Java's dominance. It was originally developed under the name LiveScript but then the marketers rather confusingly chose to get a license from Sun so they could name the language JavaScript.

This is confusing because although in theory JavaScript has a similar heritage to Java (it is an ALGOL descendant via C, Smalltalk, and Self, along with flavors of, Scheme[3]), in practice the two share little besides a name. I will not get into the boring technical details. Suffice it to say that to a programmer: JavaScript has almost nothing in common with Java.

---

[3] A marvelous language the details of which this footnote is too small to contain.

While Java was being increasingly used to write "server-side" code and "applets" that the browser would download and then launch as separate applications running in a *sandbox*[4], JavaScript slowly but surely became indispensable by virtue of the fact that it was the only language that ran *inside the browser*. Programmers could use JavaScript to write code that altered an HTML page *while it was running*.

At first this was used to do things like validation: ensuring that data was entered in a proper format, for example to make sure that people did not enter letters into a numeric field. However, it eventually became much more important. In 2005 Jesse James Garrett published *Ajax: A New Approach to Web Applications*, which gave programmers a recipe to make applet downloads obsolete.

Ajax stands for: *Asynchronous JavaScript and XML*, and the basic technique had been in use for a few years before Garrett's paper made it popular. It uses JavaScript to change a web page dynamically without re-loading all of the HTML. You may remember from Chapter 3:

> **"When you interact with a web page you are dealing with at least a dozen layers of abstraction. The "button" you click on is really**

---

[4] a digital security area *outside* of the browser

> a region of the screen which is caught by the operating system, passed to the web browser, which compares it to a map in memory which was rendered from a "Document Object Model" which was constructed by interpreting HTML (and CSS and JavaScript)"

The way Ajax works is by modifying the Document Object Model (DOM) in memory which causes the pixel rendering to change on screen without reloading the entire page.

The DOM specification has "hooks" to both Java and JavaScript, yet because JavaScript ran *inside* the browser, JavaScript had a marked advantage, and the Ajax pattern became almost universally used as the technique for creating dynamic web pages.

Netscape developed a server-side Java–Script implementation called *LiveWire Pro Web* but it never achieved the popularity of Java. But, in 2009 Ryan Dahl created a wildly successful server-side JavaScript implementation named Node.js. Since then, lots of public domain software written in JavaScript has become available. As with Java, and Objective-C before it: a rich class library of pre-written application components seems to be the key to success for a programming language.

In spite of its tremendous popularity, in my opinion there is nothing revolutionary about JavaScript either. To my eyes it is simply Yet Another Smalltalk clone with features added (admittedly some pretty weird ones) that make it all too easy to program poorly.

In the early millennium, companies like Salesforce.com were proving that it was not only possible to deliver applications over the web, but that users liked them better than the *thick applications* that had to be installed via floppy disk or CD. As IT departments adopted this technology, two tribes formed: the "back-end" dev teams that wrote in Java, and the "front-end" teams (or web integrators) that wrote in HTML, CSS, and JavaScript.

These tribes are very far apart in terms of culture, skills, and often even reporting structure, with back-end teams reporting to IT, and the front-end teams reporting to Marketing.

In recent years, many companies with a Silicon Valley or startup culture have been using JavaScript for both the front-end and the back-end (server-side). As I explain in the Introduction, these companies, and the programmers that work for them, have a very different culture from the IT departments of large public corporations in traditional sectors.

Nonetheless, server-side JavaScript using Node.js is gaining a foothold, and publicly available source code (for cutting and pasting purposes) is increasingly JavaScript code.

Whether or not this is enough to displace the installed code base of Java remains to be seen. Either way, I predict that it will make little difference. Languages come in and out of fashion with each generation of programmers. The problem of IT project failure is not affected by choice of languages.

"There does not now, nor will there ever, exist a programming language in which it is the least bit hard to write bad programs."

~ Lawrence Flon

"Enron had already collapsed and filed for bankruptcy protection by the beginning of 2002. But despite complaints from short sellers that corporations had used accounting gimmickry to inflate their profits, many investors thought the crisis at Enron was an isolated case."

~ Alex Berenson
The New York Times
January 2, 2003

Part Two

Where I explain what happened since 1990 to create the mess we are in today.

How business people became frustrated with IT and stopped funding IT projects, and how that failed, and changes in accounting practices brought programming back in-house.

How programmers were on the verge of making it better…

How headline making corporate and accounting scandals led to the Sarbanes–Oxley Act of 2002…

…and how the Gartner Group, and the Project management Institute inadvertently set programming back 20 years.

"Humans are pattern-seeking, story-telling animals and we are quite adept at telling stories about patterns whether they exist or not."

~ Michael Shermer

Chapter Six
Crisis

Revenge of the business managers

By the early nineties, business people's attitude towards computing had undergone a radical transformation.

Before the ubiquity of desktop personal computers – PCs – computing had been a magical process that took place on a mysterious floor of the office building onto which very few people were allowed. It was called the glass house.

Typical "glass house" computer room, notice glass wall to the right

The department responsible for the glass house was almost always part of Finance, and was called Management Information Services (MIS), not Information Technologies (IT). It would be difficult for anyone who entered the workplace after 1990 to understand just how remote and out of sight computers used to be.

There is a very old joke circulating in the programmer community. It is a list of ways to shoot yourself in the foot using different programming languages (the premise being that all programmers eventually shoot themselves in the foot, so it is handy to have a list of how to do it). The list is now long, and the style of the entries has changed a lot, but when it first started circulating, the list was relatively short and had a definite style. Each way to shoot yourself in the foot was described in code. And each one contained an obvious, but hilarious, syntactical error that would result in some terrible doom for the hapless programmer. However, the entry for IBM Job Control Language (JCL) had no code or pseudo code in it, yet it speaks volumes:

> **You send your foot down to MIS and include a 300-page document explaining exactly how you want it to be shot. Two years later, your foot comes back deep-fried.**

People did not look forward to dealing with MIS. It was perceived as difficult and unproductive. PCs changed everything.

Power to the people

IBM introduced the PC in 1981 and after a decade, personal computers had become a commonplace sight in the office. Demand for personal programs was a logical outgrowth.

Not only had seeing PCs on people's desks slowly eroded the aura of mystery surrounding computers but now there was even "shrink wrapped" software. Programs like spreadsheets and word processors written by professional programmers were sold in computer stores in cellophane wrapped boxes that contained "floppy" disks with which users could install the program on their own computers. Remember: before this point, the only way business department users could get a program written for them was to "send their foot down to MIS with a 300-page document".

And PCs had more than just spreadsheets and word processors.

When IBM planned the PC, it had in mind a technically inclined user. Because of this they commissioned a piece of software from a company named Ashton-Tate. The software was dBase II, and it was a database.

With a database, you could get rid of mountains of paper. Offices in those days were littered with paper - mostly lists. Lists of the phone extensions of all the people in the company, lists of suppliers and their phone numbers, lists and "rolodexes" of customers' addresses, lists and then lists again.

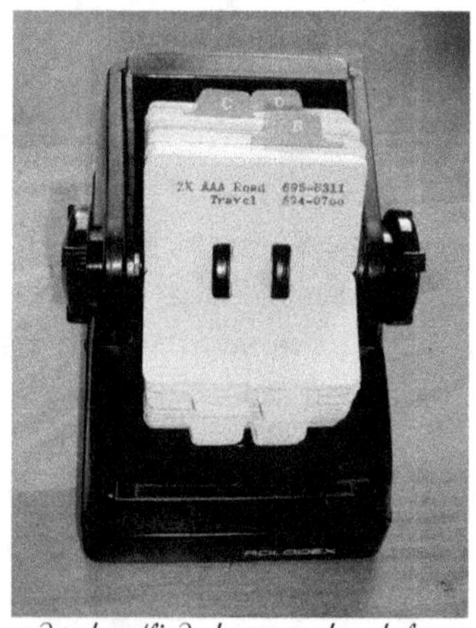

How people used to keep/find phone numbers before mobile phones

A database could hold all of those lists, and let you look at them on screen whenever you needed to.

dBase II was among the first *4th generation languages* (4GLs), so called because they are one abstraction level up from 3GLs such as Pascal or C. When the IBM PC went on sale, dBase was one of the few shrink-wrapped programs immediately available, and it was a runaway success. Long before Microsoft was a household word, Ashton-Tate was the biggest software publisher in the industry.

dBase II included a pre-built database engine and screen renderer, and its own language for accessing the database, creating business logic, and drawing screens. Here is an example of dBase:

```
USE empl
REPLACE ALL salary WITH salary * 1.1 FOR supervisors > 0
LIST ALL fname, lname, salary TO PRINT
```

I think that most people can probably figure out what is going on with this code even if they are not programmers. We are using a table of employees, we are giving all supervisors a 10% raise, and we are printing out the full list of employees and their salaries.

To code this in a 3GL would be tens of thousands of lines at least. Each line of dBase code rests upon thousands of lines of 3GL code that perform the functions described with one word of dBase.

4GLs were obviously tremendous productivity enhancers. But they did give rise to problems of their own. With thousands of amateur programmers writing software that ran their businesses, it was not unusual for some to get in over their heads. Many were the times that IT departments were asked to "fix" an application that had been originally coded by an amateur in a 4GL and was now starting to break under the strain of too much data, or the need for multi-user access, or sometimes just basic programming mistakes.

When I was the chief technology officer (CTO) of a large organization I had to have a policy about this. Like most other large organizations of that era, we had a few cases where computers supporting millions of dollars of business were running under someone's desk where a power failure or a careless cleaner could corrupt the data and cause weeks or months of work. My policy was this: no fixes or support for 4GL databases, only rewrites, in a "real" programming language. It's not that the 4GLs weren't great, I personally spent many happy hours writing programs in a half dozen different ones. They just couldn't handle enterprise scale.

Below are just a few of the very popular 4GLs that were used by industrious employees to create business applications and by vertical market specialists writing special purpose applications for (usually) small market niches:

- DBase
- Clipper
- Foxbase
- MS Access
- Filemaker
- HyperCard
- PowerBuilder
- Uniface
- Omnis
- Informix
- Progress
- 4th[th] Dimension

The impact of these programs was dramatic. Programming was in some sense returning to its roots as an avocation, something that smart motivated people did in order to advance their primary field of interest. This time, instead of academics writing programs for research, it was business people writing programs to automate manual office tasks. For example, "mail merge", the ability to select from a list of names and addresses and print out a form letter with the names and addresses filled in automatically was a very big deal. It sounds very trivial today, when most people carry around a computer in their pocket, and all mail is e-mail, but in those days of paper letters and envelopes, it saved hours, sometimes days of labor. It was like magic, and it was something that MIS would never have done because their time and their machines were too expensive to justify working on solving such a small (to them) problem. PCs represented freedom from the tyranny of MIS, and part of that freedom was the freedom to write one's own programs.

And for the business people too busy or simply not inclined to learn a 4GL, it was still clear to them that customized programs could be written quickly and inexpensively for their personal computers by any one of an army of independent contractors (like me) vying for the opportunity.

If at first, you don't succeed… you must be in IT

It was during this decade that MIS started to rebrand itself IT, and IT project failures started attracting attention.

In late 1988, *Business Week* published an article that stated a "survey of 600 firms indicated that 35% of them had at least one 'runaway' software project"[32]. Soon after, Dr. Barry Boehm, the Director of the U.S. Department of Defense's Advanced Research Projects Agency published a series of articles about software risk management which further raised awareness about failed software projects.

---

[32] Rothfeder, Jeffrey, *It's Late, Costly, Incompetent – But Try Firing a Computer System*. Business Week, November 7, 1988.

The Project Management Institute (PMI) had been working very hard to elevate project management to a profession with standards and practices that could be considered equal to that of engineering. As part of this effort, studies were instituted on projects of all sorts, and for the next few years reports started emerging with statistics on software development project success/failure rates. They were not encouraging[33].

Finally, two very influential reports came out in 1994: The Standish Group's *Chaos Report*[34], and KPMG's *Report on IT Runaway Systems*[35], each of which independently surveyed large companies with large IT projects (in the US and the UK respectively). Both reported that in the opinion of the executives surveyed, barely a third of their IT projects could be considered definite successes. The failure of in-house custom software development projects was becoming well documented and corporate executives, especially executives of public

---

[33] The Project Management Institute estimated that North American companies lost "nearly $300 billion on late, overbudget, or failed implementations during 1999–2001"

[34] Standish Group International. The Chaos Report; www.standish-group.com/sample_ research/PDFpages/Chaos1994.pdf.

[35] KPMG. Report on IT Runaway Systems. [Online]. Strategys for KPMG Management Consulting, 1994. [16/02/2017]. Available from: eis.mdx.ac.uk/research/SFC/Reports/KPMG_ITsystems.pdf

corporations, were confronted with the responsibility of having to seek solutions to prevent the waste of shareholder's money (estimated by both Standish and the PMI to be in the billions) as auditors increasingly focused on IT spending.

There were four different responses to this burgeoning crisis from four different communities: computer scientists (and software engineers), project managers, IT managers, and business managers. Over the next few chapters I will tell you about each one.

The academics, computer scientists, and software engineers naturally took scientific approaches: gathering data, proposing hypotheses, and then testing them through experimentation. The result of this was an explosion of proposed methodologies claiming to address the root causes of IT project failures. We will go into these in the very next chapter.

The project managers took the most practical approach possible, building on the existing de facto process (known as the waterfall method and also discussed in the next chapter) to address the concerns of the auditors and the finance department. It bears remembering that many corporate IT departments were still reporting to the CFO at this time. Project management also has a chapter to itself, Chapter Eight.

IT managers reacted defensively. The *Chaos Report*'s first paragraph referred to a paper co-authored by the computer scientist Alfred Spector.[36]

> **"In 1986, Alfred Spector, president of Transarc Corporation, co-authored a paper comparing bridge building to software development. The premise: Bridges are normally built on-time, on- budget, and do not fall down.**
>
> **....**
>
> **One of the biggest reasons bridges come in on-time, on-budget and do not fall down is because of the extreme detail of design. The design is frozen and the contractor has little flexibility in changing the specifications. "**

IT managers did not have to be told twice, and the quest to nail down specifications became an absolute mania. To my dismay, IT managers rushed to become "the department of No", often taking a truculently defiant stance that no estimates would be issued, no commitments made, until the internal business client signed in blood that the requirements were set in stone and complete.

---

[36] https://www.projectsmart.co.uk/white-papers/chaos-report.pdf

I saw this as a fast track to marginalization and insignificance because as the *Chaos Report* also pointed out on the same page:

> "…in today's fast moving business environment, a frozen design does not accommodate changes in the business practice".

Commercial Off the Shelf

I was not wrong. The nineties became a time of unprecedented friction between IT and the business units within companies, and this brings us to the response of the business managers and auditors.

Just as freezing requirements became an obsession for IT managers, bypassing IT completely became a fixation for many business managers. With the success of the PC and shrink-wrapped software they figured they had the tools to do it. COTS became the buzzword of the day. It is an acronym for Commercial Off The Shelf, and the idea was that eliminating internal development projects would eliminate project failures. Let a third party assume the risk went the thinking. If they fail to deliver, then we don't pay them. The company is protected. This philosophy was very closely aligned to the overall business trend towards outsourcing and suited the purchasing department and the auditors just fine, thank you very much. No less a personage than Fred Brooks endorsed the idea. For a number of years at the end of the nineties and the early years of the millennium, the policy of purchasing COTS instead of opting for internal program development was anointed *best practice* and pursued aggressively.

This trend hit its peak during the time I was CTO of a large international organization. Every other week, I was meeting with an external software vendor who had been brought in by a business manager in an attempt to do an end run around IT only to be brought up short when they discovered a need to integrate with in-house systems.

Unlike many other IT managers, I was not hostile to these vendors. I tried to be tough but fair. I was fundamentally sympathetic to the business users' desire to cut me out. I was the representative of a department that seemed to take a perverse delight in thwarting even the slightest progress, patiently lecturing in the most condescending of tones that business needed "to understand" this, that or the other thing, or "that's just not the way it works," or just like the building contractor tells you about your kitchen renovations, "you can have it fast, good, or cheap, but not all three".

James H. Boren's delightful adage from his legendary work *When in Doubt, Mumble* is:

"Bureaucracy is the epoxy that greases the wheels of progress,"[37]

I used to joke that I was an international bureaucrat, and it was my job to prevent things from happening. But in reality, I deplored the attempts of my colleagues to make business conform to the limits that IT lacked the courage to surpass. I felt, as I always have and still do, that technology has no relevance if it is not used in service of some human pursuit such as the pursuit of business. I wanted my department to push whatever technology or process boundaries it needed to in order to keep up with the demands of the market and the need of the business to stay competitive.

I successfully pushed for a reorganization that moved IT *Business* Solutions into a separate team from that of the glass house so we could be free of their foot-dragging and no-but-isms. I deliberately had the IT Business Solutions team act just as a third-party software vendor would. I bid competitively against the external vendors the business managers brought in. I tried to win on merit, not

---

[37] Boren, James H. *When In Doubt, Mumble*. New York [Etc.], Van Nostrand Reinhold, 1972.

hegemony. I placed my Business Solution Managers in the departments they served and drilled them to never respond to an idea with the type of passive-aggressive statements that the other IT managers insisted their team members use. Phrases such as "It might be very difficult…" and "it could be very complicated" and the infamous "you have to understand…" were replaced by "that sounds like a good idea, let's see what it would take to make that work" or "I think I understand why you want to go in that direction. Can I just play it back to you to make sure I do?"

But my efforts notwithstanding, the *best practices* of the purchasing department and auditors saw to it that for several years the COTS vendors did very well, selling systems to business managers who signed contracts in blissful ignorance of the fate that awaited them.

The ultimate outcome of the COTS fad was tragically predictable because large public companies all have two things in common.

First, all of them have entirely unique, byzantine processes that are sacred and totally unchangeable because of corporate culture. Large companies have strange ways of doing things. One large company I worked at (a multibillion-dollar corporation) took Gross

Revenues, deducted only commissions (not any of the other costs) and called it Net Revenue – not exactly what the rest of the world understands by that term. My favorite was the organization that created Northern Asia and Southern Asia as two territories and then declared Singapore to be in Northern Asia. So mighty were we, that even the earth's geography would bend to our will. These are just a few *small* examples of the separate reality that large corporations live in.

Second, they all evaluate expenditures as being driven by one of only two possible motivations: They make investments either to get ahead of the competition, or so as not to get left behind by the industry.

When an innovation occurs (technical or any other kind), a few adventurous, risk-tolerant executives will seize on it to get ahead of the competition. Therefore, they want to build in-house to keep things proprietary. This is a relatively cost-insensitive endeavor. As long as the cost is a reasonable percentage of the revenues it generates, no further attention is paid. Growth is more important than cost control.

When enough other companies have copied the innovation, it is no longer a competitive advantage and the adventurous executives completely lose interest in it. Companies that join the trend late benefit from low prices because third-party vendors will have entered the market making it a commodity. The conservative, risk averse executives that inherit responsibility for the early in-house innovations feel pressure to abandon expensive proprietary implementations in order to bring their costs down to the same level as that enjoyed by the late comers. They will then seek a cookie cutter solution (ideally maintained by a third party) at the lowest possible cost. All innovations suffer this fate; the line is constantly being redrawn. Today's precious proprietary technology is tomorrow's boat anchor. Like some sharks, companies have to keep moving or they will suffocate.

The COTS strategy is suitable for these late-stage situations where a technology is no longer a competitive advantage. Everyone is happy with a cookie cutter solution as long as it keeps costs to a bare minimum.

However, for dealing with unique corporate culture and processes, or the desire for proprietary competitive features, COTS is an utter failure. The whole premise of COTS and the basis of its success is that it is cookie cutter. Trying to customize it is a recipe for disaster, and it is a recipe that serves generous portions.

Disasters with COTS customization projects became legendary, even more prone to spectacular failure than internal custom development.

COTS fell out of vogue on the heels of a string of highly publicized multi-million dollar failures such as the 1993 shipping and inventory catastrophes that brought drug company FoxMeyer and appliance maker Whirlpool to bankruptcy court with SAP, and the dire shortage of Hershey's Kisses and Jolly Ranchers on the shelves for Halloween 1999 after Hershey tried to implement COTS software from SAP, Seibel, and Manugistics.

After a number of these debacles, there was simply no way that anyone could conceivably continue to call it *best* practice to buy COTS unless the intention was to use it *exactly* as-is. This coincided with some very significant changes to accounting rules, and between the two things, in-house custom development suddenly came very much back into fashion.

Three-card Monte

There are going to be a lot of acronyms in the next two pages, and I apologize for that. But I feel it is important to document the assertions I will be making in Chapter Eight with facts that you can look up for yourself to see that I am not making this up out of thin air.

This part of our story focuses on the alterations to accounting rules that changed everything, and it involves two professional associations: The *Financial Accounting Standards Board* (FASB) and the *American Institute of CPAs* (AICPA).

Up until this point, there was a general sense amongst accounting professionals that software development for internal use (any software that was not offered to customers for purchase) was similar in nature to R&D efforts, and as such, should be expensed as incurred as per *Statement of Financial Accounting Standards* (SFAS) No. 2. However, there were no specific prescriptive regulations, and so companies were free to interpret. Most companies did indeed expense internal-use software development. However, some companies were beginning to account for internal-use software development as a capital expenditure. As a result, the *Securities and Exchange Commission* (SEC) began to receive pressure to establish regulations because "a trend was developing in accounting practices that was having an adverse effect on financial statement comparability". [38]

What this rather diplomatic statement means in plain language is that some public companies were gaining *unfair advantage* by choosing to capitalize internal-use software. This is because all publicly traded companies use double entry bookkeeping. In this system money leaving the bank account to pay for salaries of developers must have a *balancing* entry and *where* that balancing entry is made can have a big impact on the company's financial picture.

Companies that treated software development as R&D created a balancing entry in the *Expense* area of their chart of accounts. This had the effect of lowering profits.

Companies that capitalized software development made the balancing entry in the *Assets* area of their chart of accounts. This had the dual effect of raising profits *and* making the company more valuable on paper.

It is not hard to see why the CFO of a public company would prefer to do the latter, and

---

[38] Thomas, 1983;
https://www.sec.gov/news/speech/1983/050583thomas.pdf

a few of the more aggressive ones were doing it. The less aggressive ones were complaining and asking for the SEC to either stop the practice altogether, or level the playing field by giving clear permission for *everyone* to start doing it.

In 1994, the staff of the SEC asked the FASB Emerging Issues Task Force (EITF) to develop financial reporting guidance for internal-use software. After discussion with AICPA, it was agreed that AICPA's policy group AcSEC should handle the project because "it was able to provide the necessary due process, including exposure for public comment, that such a broad project warrants".[39] The result was released four years later as *Statement of Position* (SOP) 98-1. As we shall see in Chapter Eight, this guideline was to become the single most influential, yet least recognized, influence on software application development practices of the 21st century.

---

[39] Ameen & Noll 1997; "Accounting for the Costs of Computer Software Developed or Obtained for Internal Use," http://www.journalofaccountancy.com/issues/1997/mar/news.html

"Capital isn't this pile of money sitting somewhere; it's an accounting construct".

~Bethany McLean[40]

---

[40] Goodkind, Nicole, and Daily Ticker. "Bank Capital Is An Illusion: Bethany Mclean". *Finance.Yahoo.Com*, 2014, https://finance.yahoo.com/blogs/daily-ticker/bank-capital-is-an-illusion--bethany-mclean-080136954.html.

Chapter Seven
Breakthrough

While business managers and auditors were conducting their COTS experiment, computer scientists and software engineers tackled the problem of IT project failures by proposing new methodologies. A dozen methodologies emerged in the nineties.

A software development methodology is a *model* of a process that defines the steps to follow to create applications. It usually separates the steps into phases and may define specific deliverables or artifacts. In the beginning, methods were imposed by the limitations of the hardware. The cycle of writing code, keying it onto a punch card, feeding it into a batch, getting and analyzing the results, was a methodology unto itself. It was only after programmers could interact directly with the compiler, in real time, that there was enough freedom to pursue the methodologies we will review in this chapter.

We will start from the base that Brooks established in *The Mythical Man-Month*. That method was generally known as the "waterfall" method because it assumed that the phases of development followed each other in strict sequence with little or no overlap.

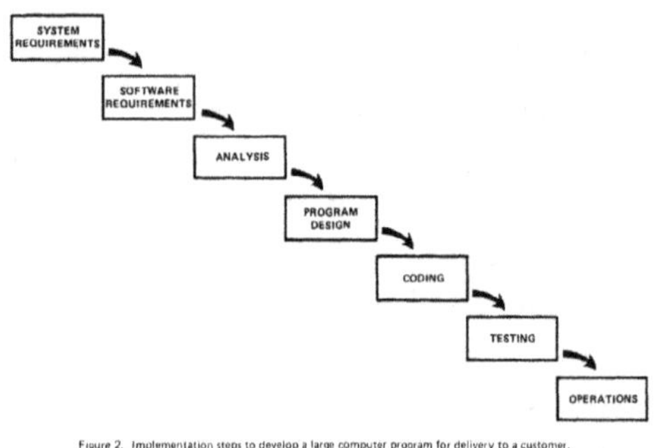

Figure 2. Implementation steps to develop a large computer program for delivery to a customer.

Like any human endeavor, each generation sought to improve upon the previous. The next step towards the age of methodologies was in the mid-eighties. Barry Boehm published *A Spiral Model of Software Development and Enhancement* in response to the concern expressed in a 1987 report authored by Dr. Brooks that "traditional software process models were discouraging more effective approaches to software development such as prototyping and software reuse".[1] Boehm puts it so well, I will simply quote him:

---

1   [1] F.P. Brooks et al., *Defense Science Board Task Force Report on Military Software*, Office of the Under Secretary of Defense for Acquisition, Washington, DC 20301, Sept. 1987.

"A primary source of difficulty with the waterfall model has been its emphasis on fully elaborated documents as completion criteria for early requirements and design phases. For some classes of software, such as compilers or secure operating systems, this is the most effective way to proceed. However, it does not work well for many classes of software, particularly interactive end-user applications. Document-driven standards have pushed many projects to write elaborate specifications of poorly understood user interfaces and decision support functions, followed by the design and development of large quantities of unusable code".[2]

The key phrases are: *"fully elaborated documents as completion criteria"* and *"Document-driven standards"*. He is talking about the Business Requirements Documents which hyper-defensive IT departments demand internal business clients sign in blood to ensure that the requirements are set in stone and will never change — as if such a thing were even possible in a fast-moving business environment!

It is astonishing and depressing that thirty years later enterprise IT still considers it standard (if not best) practice to "write elaborate specifications of poorly understood user

---

[2] Boehm, B. W. "A Spiral Model Of Software Development And Enhancement". *Computer*, vol 21, no. 5, 1988, pp. 61-72. *Institute Of Electrical And Electronics Engineers (IEEE)*, doi:10.1109/2.59.

interfaces and decision support functions, followed by the design and development of large quantities of unusable code".

The spiral model is based on the idea also expounded in *The Mythical Man-Month* that the first release of a program will never be completely satisfactory. Brooks advocates planning "to throw one away". Boehm suggests instead a series of prototypes, investing incrementally more effort with each cycle. It bears mention that the same idea was propounded in slightly different language by Royce in 1970. As I said before, Royce did not invent, nor did he promote, waterfall. His primary concern was how to overcome its limitations by introducing iteration, and Boehm's work was a continuation of that.

But Boehm was of a previous generation. A newer generation was wrestling with the same issues but wanted an approach that integrated the technological advances of Object-Oriented Programming (OOP).

When I first started to program in OOP, I really struggled to understand analysis and design for object-oriented programming. One couldn't really just start programming the way you could with earlier languages. There were decisions to be made before you even started.

The analysis was different from what program-mers like me were used to.

Many programmers were already used to carefully modeling their data. There was a high "cost" to getting the data model wrong, it was difficult to migrate the data to a new structure, and it was a chore to keep track of all the code that needed to be changed. Time spent up front to get it right was time well spent. Just as the master carpenter advised: "Measure twice cut once". In addition, the data model tended to inform the program design, which made it easier to jump in and start coding.

However, programming in an object-oriented language required some thought about classes (the templates that are used to create objects). When I first started, I was trying to create what programmers call *domain-specific* class libraries. In other words, I was trying to create classes to fit the real-world business functions of whatever application I was building.

Ground Zero

By now the attentive reader may have noticed a pattern: Significant advances in compu-ting tend to "take hold" about a decade after the initial innovation, sometimes a bit longer. I first struggled with OOP in 1986. Academic computer scientists and software engineers researched and proposed theories for ten years. I finally got my first answers in 1996 when I happened across something called *WikiWiki-Web*.

Yes, *that* wiki. The same thing Wikipedia is built on.

WikiWikiWeb was the first one, and it was the personal/professional website of the Wiki inventor, Ward Cunningham[3]. Cunningham is less well-known than many of his contemporaries but no less talented or influential. In his own words, he has dedicated himself to "improving the effectiveness of technical experts, mostly by creating new computer tools, but also by radically simplifying methods". He adds almost as an afterthought: "I am most well-known for my contributions to object-oriented design, agile methodology, and collaborative software".[4]

Humble words for someone who has given so much to so many people. He may be the

---

[3] Wiki is Hawaiian for quick (wiki wiki meaning *very* quick) and Cunningham thought it sounded cooler than Quick Web which was his first idea.

[4] "Ward Cunningham's Profile". *Linkedin*, 2017, https://www.linkedin.com/in/wardcunningham/.

most important programmer you have never heard of. Cunningham's contributions to computing, and to the world at large, are certainly as important as anyone else in the industry.

The ACM had an annual conference called OOPSLA (Object-Oriented Programming, Systems, Languages & Applications). The innovators in methodology participated in this conference, but for the rest of the year, many of them were corresponding on WikWikiWeb, sometimes known by its domain name *c2.com*. It is still up and running and is like an online computing museum. It can give you glimpse of what websites looked like in 1995.

Welcome Visitors

Welcome to the WikiWikiWeb, also known as "Wiki". A lot of people had their first wiki experience here. This community has been around since 1995 and consists of many people. We always accept newcomers with valuable contributions. If you haven't used a wiki before, be prepared for a bit of CultureShock. The usefulness of Wiki is in the freedom, simplicity, and power it offers.

This site's primary focus is PeopleProjectsAndPatterns in SoftwareDevelopment. However, it is more than just an InformalHistoryOfProgrammingIdeas. It started there, but the theme has created a culture and DramaticIdentity all its own. All Wiki content is WorkInProgress. Most of all, this is a forum where people share ideas! It changes as people come and go. Much of the information here is subjective. If you are looking for a dedicated reference site, try WikiPedia; WikiIsNotWikipedia!

This was where I became familiar with the work of Cunningham, Kent Beck, Grady Booch, James Rumbaugh, and Ivar Jacobson all of whom I will tell you about in a minute. It was also where I one day saw the page below:

ScrumPages

Rugby players *scrum* when they surround the ball and move it forward together. The word has been borrowed to describe a collective form of software development that is claimed to be distinctly different from traditional processes including waterfall, spiral and iterative development. These are pages where one can learn more about the scrum...

- http://www.tiac.net/users/virman/ap.htm
- http://www.controlchaos.com/scrumwp.htm
- http://www.tiac.net/users/jsuth/objwld96/ind3scru.html

and related issues ...

- http://www.stlabs.com/real_01.htm

EditText of this page (last edited November 7, 1996)
FindPage by browsing or searching

Which led me to this website:

SCRUM Software Development Process

Building The Best Possible Software

"The problem for engineers is that change translates into chaos, especially when a single error can potentially bring down an entire system. But, change also translates into opportunity. It's as simple as this: if there is time to put a certain amount of functionality into the product easily, then there is time to put in more functionality at the price of a certain amount of disruption and risk. Thus does madness creep into our projects - we will tend to take on as much risk as we possibly can."

James Bach. October 1995. 'American Programmer'

Copyright 1995 Advanced Development Methods All Rights Reserved

Contents

- Introduction
- Overview
- Current Development Situation
- Methodology
- Phases
- Controls
- Deliverables
- Project Team
- Characteristics
- Advantages
- Estimating
- Appendix 1 - System Development Methodologies : Defined or Empirical

Introduction

In this paper we introduce a development process, SCRUM, that treats major portions of systems development as a controlled black box. We relate this to complexity theory to show why this approach increases flexibility and ability to deal with complexity, and produces a system that is responsive to both initial and additionally occurring requirements.

When I started reading WikiWikiWeb in 1996, I had accidentally stumbled into ground zero of the most influential software development movement of the 21st century: Agile.

Triumvirate

Before I get to what I learned about Agile, I first want to talk about the Rational Software Corporation, and the influence of the Object Management Group. At the time, it seemed bigger and more important than Agile.

Since it was clear to everybody that OOP was here to stay, several large companies felt that establishing some standards around OOP would benefit everyone involved. In 1989 they formed the Object Management Group (OMG). The founding members were mainly computer manufacturers; Apple Computer, Hewlett-Packard, IBM, Phillips, Unisys, Sun Microsystems and Data General. For ten years, they focused on standards for creating objects that could *inter-operate* across different languages and different platforms. This was of concern to them, but it didn't really address the core of the challenge facing programmers like me, which was how to analyze the business problem and create an object model that fit it.

Grady Booch was Chief Scientist of Rational Software for 30 years from its founding in 1981 through its acquisition by IBM.[5] He

---

[5] In 2008 became Chief Scientist, Software Engineering in IBM Research. (Wikipedia)

had his first programming experience on an IBM 1130, a computer so small (by IBM standards) that it was used as a mere connector between the two-million dollar IBM System/360 and its equally expensive 2250 Graphics Display Unit. Because it was so "inexpensive" it was many a young programmer's "first computer". Here is the story in his own words:

> **"... I pounded the doors at the local IBM sales office until a salesman took pity on me. After we chatted for a while, he handed me a Fortran [manual]. I'm sure he gave it to me thinking, "I'll never hear from this kid again". I returned the following week saying, "This is really cool. I've read the whole thing and have written a small program. Where can I find a computer?" The fellow, to my delight, found me programming time on an IBM 1130 on weekends and late-evening hours. That was my first programming experience, and I must thank that anonymous IBM salesman for launching my career. Thank you, IBM".[6]**

In 1994 Booch published *Object Oriented Analysis and Design with Applications*[7], and in it he presented the Booch Method that combined

---

[6] Grady Booch (2003-04-03) in interview "*Grady Booch polishes his crystal ball*", IBM

[7] Booch, Grady. *Object-Oriented Analysis And Design With Applications*. Reading, Massachusetts, Addison-Wesley, 1994.

prescriptions for analysis, an object-modeling language (a standardized set of symbols used to model a software system), an iterative development process similar to Boehm's spiral method, and a set of recommended practices. He was an active member of OOPSLA, and he collaborated with Ward Cunningham, which was how I first became aware of his work.

James (Jim) Rumbaugh is a computer scientist who worked as a researcher for thirty years, first at Digital Equipment Corporation (they made the PDP and VAX minicomputers), and then at General Electric. There he led the creation of a methodology called Object-modeling technique. In 1994 he joined Rational Software and worked with Grady Booch to merge the two methods.

One year later, the telecom company Ericsson sold one of its divisions to Rational. The division was the brainchild of Ivar Jacobson who came along with it to Rational He was another computer scientist creating an object-oriented methodology. His was called Object-Oriented Software Engineering and is the origin of the popular term "use case"[8].

---

[8] Wikipedia: In software and systems engineering, a *use case* is a list of actions or event steps typically defining the interactions between a role (known in the Unified Modeling Language as an actor) and a

The minds behind three of the top five methodologies were working together at Rational to meld their approaches as Unified Modeling Language (UML) and the Rational Unified Process (RUP), and not long after that the other two[9] joined forces with them to contributed to UML.

After seeing the specifications for UML, the OMG decided to solicit proposals for a unified object method that they could adopt as a standard. The Rational proposal had broad support from OMG members and in short order they selected and adopted UML.

For a brief shining moment, it really seemed as though the computer industry was going to agree on a successor to the waterfall method that would make everything better. All of the major computer companies endorsed UML and RUP, which offered real improvements. Enterprise IT started to sign up to the idea, and things were starting to get better.

But as I will explain in the next chapter, some of the smartest people in the world were

---

system to achieve a goal. The actor can be a human or other external system.

[9] Steve Mellor and Sally Shlaer, authors of Object-Oriented Systems Analysis (OOSA), and Peter Coad co-author of Object-oriented analysis (OOA)

about to be thwarted by plodding bean counters. But just before I do that, I want to write about Agile.

Where the rubber meets the road

The researchers I just mentioned were focused on formal analysis and design methods. At the same time the OOPSLA/WikiWikiWeb community was also home to a loose affiliation of practitioners less interested in pure theory, and much more interested in practical application, asking – as Ward Cunningham suggested – "What's the simplest thing that could possibly work?" They were very interested in figuring out ways to apply lessons learned in manufacturing and industrial design.

In early 2001, seventeen of these practitioners assembled at a ski lodge in Snowbird, Utah to discuss "lightweight" processes and methodologies[10]. They were a diverse group, so these were loose terms. In fact, at least one of them, Martin Fowler, "didn't expect much at that meeting".[11] Interviews with other attendees suggest that none of them did, and that the prevailing sentiment was similar to

---

[10] As opposed to documentation driven, heavyweight software development processes

[11] https://martinfowler.com/articles/agileStory.html

Martin's, that "we would get to know each other better and that greater communication would lead to something interesting".

I have already introduced you to Ward Cunningham and Kent Beck. They were there. Along with Ron Jeffries they had created XP, the Extreme Programming method in 1996.

Jeff Sutherland and Ken Schwaber, the inventors of the Scrum software development process, were there with Mike Beedle who formed the world's second Scrum team and co-wrote the first book on Scrum with Schwaber.

James Grenning who invented planning poker, used extensively by Scrum teams, and popular authors Andy Hunt, and Dave Thomas attended. Jim Highsmith, founding member of The Agile Alliance came too.

And last but not least Robert Cecil Martin – Uncle Bob – was there encouraging the rest of them to create and sign a manifesto (at Ward Cunningham's suggestion).

And that is exactly what they did. Here are Jon Kern's notes, scribbled on a printout of the agenda that had been posted on WikiWikiWeb prior to the meeting[12].

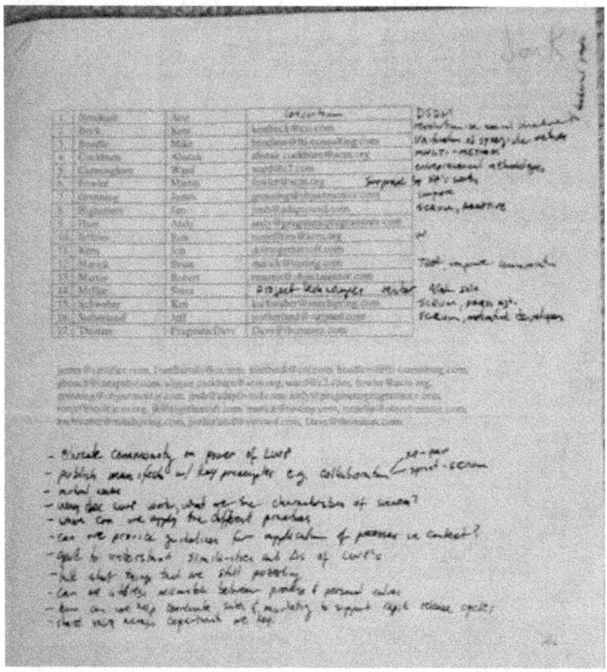

The Agile movement is so varied and rich that it would take an entire book (or two) to do it justice. I simply cannot do it here. All I can say is that Agile has attracted the best minds of computer science and software engineering, and I have been a loyal adherent of it since I

---

[12] With thanks to Jon Kern for sharing this on his website. http://www.scruminc.com/wp-content/uploads/2016/01/AgileManifestoNotes2001.pdf

read my first WikiWikiWeb entry on XP. Which is why it pains me so much to say none of the Agile methods have moved the needle on reducing IT project failure.

It seems that Agile was working on a different set of challenges (in which it succeeds very well): continuous improvement, master craftsmanship, self-organizing teams, and team dynamics.

As for the subject of this book: Agile had its chance, and it is very clearly not the cure for IT project failure.

Manifesto for Agile Software Development

We are uncovering better ways of developing software by doing it and helping others do it. Through this work we have come to value:

Individuals and interactions over processes and tools

Working software over comprehensive documentation

Customer collaboration over contract negotiation

Responding to change over following a plan

That is, while there is value in the items on the right, we value the items on the left more.

Kent Beck

Mike Beedle

Arie van Bennekom

Alistair Cockburn

Ward Cunningham

Martin Fowler

James Grenning

Jim Highsmith

Andrew Hunt

Ron Jeffries

Jon Kern

Brian Marick

Robert C. Martin

Steve Mellor

Ken Schwaber

Jeff Sutherland

Dave Thomas

"But I should caution that if you seek to plot out all your moves before you make them—if you put your faith in slow, deliberative planning in the hopes it will spare you failure down the line—well, you're deluding yourself."

— Ed Catmull, Pixar

Chapter Eight
Letdown

You can't go back ...

The last words I wrote in Chapter 5 were:

The result was released four years later as *Statement of Position* (SOP) 98-1. As we shall see in Chapter 8, this guideline was to generate the single most influential, yet least recognized, impact on application development practices of the 21st century

In 2004, I left the world of corporate IT to spend seven years working with startups and VCs as a positioning expert. I helped companies find the best market niches for their technologies and helped them to market themselves successfully in those niches.

2004 was a time of great optimism in the IT field. The web was new technology. E-commerce was raising our profile and giving us an opportunity to get out of the basement and into the boardroom. We had object-oriented languages that were going to promote software reuse. Model-driven architecture and CASE tools[1] were going to automate software production and make it align better with business. It seemed that Computer Science and Software Engineering were passing from a Renaissance period to the modern era. The Three Amigos (Booch, Rumbaugh, and Jacobson) had unified object-oriented analysis and design, and Microsoft and IBM were both on board. Soon the whole world would be doing iterative development and rapid prototyping, and all would be well.

In 2004, I was unaware of SOP-98. It had not yet made itself felt. I had heard vague mutterings about something called Stage-Gate process from my project managers, but they were clerks and bureaucrats, paper pushers. Not even a *necessary* evil, just a *convenient* one. They kept the Gannt charts updated and the company officers off my back.

As I said, I was away working with startups for seven years. When I returned in 2011, things were very different. Because of Stage-Gate[2], what I saw upon my return were: Web–based applications collapsing under their own weight; Code quality driven down to the

---

[1] I didn't even get around to telling you about those two things yet. But I will in Part Four.

[2] I will explain shortly.

lowest common denominator; Millions of dollars spent on architecture that was promptly ignored by the development teams. I saw the waterfall method applied brutally, without regard
to its insufficiencies, inefficiencies, or ineffec-
tiveness. I saw Agile being used as a club to
beat developers at daily standup meetings that
were about as far from Agile as you could get.
And everywhere I saw hopelessly fictitious
project plans being presented as truth. I saw
despair, not the hope that was present in 2004.

It turned me into an investigator. For
years I collected data. I interviewed my colleagues. I spoke to project managers, programmers, comptrollers, directors of project management offices (PMOs) and project control
offices (PCOs). I needed to know what could
have possibly happened to motivate people
who knew better to throw away decades of
progress and go back to discredited practices
from more than thirty years previous. In time,
I pieced it together, and that is why I am writing this book.

Gathering clouds

What had happened? The mumblings
about Stage-Gate which I had ignored had
been a harbinger of doom I had failed to recognize. It was the "nose of the camel" entering the

tent. Before describing it however, it's necessary to set the stage.

In late 2004, the giant IT analyst firm Gartner announced its impending acquisition of a smaller competitor, the META Group. META's Vice President Enterprise Planning was Robert A. Handler. He specialized in IT Project and Portfolio Management (PPM). Just as Gartner was acquiring META, Handler was co-authoring a book with one of his customers – Bryan Maizlish, IT Program Director of Lockeed Martin.

In April 2005, in the same month that Gartner completed its acquisition of META, John Wiley & Sons published *IT Portfolio Management Step-by-Step: Unlocking the Business Value of Technology*, authored by Handler and Maizlish. Gartner was quick to adopt this book and to promote its practices. Research published by Gartner on *IT Portfolio Management* was almost twice what it had been for the four previous years. In 2006 it had actually doubled, and by 2007 it had tripled.

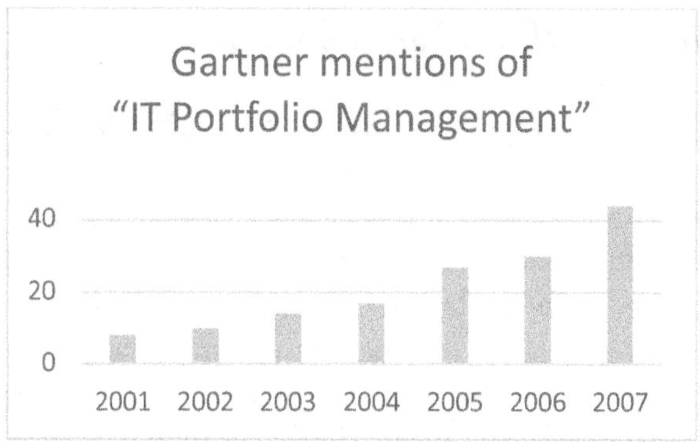

CIO Magazine was pushing too, with more articles dedicated to or prominently mentioning IT Portfolio Management between 2005 and 2007 then in all other years put together.

Why does this matter? Let's consider two of the main concerns of PPM:

Governance. In particular a rigorous process for approval of project funding designed to evaluate return on investment, and...

Compliance with the Sarbanes–Oxley Act of 2002 (SOX), which had been passed as a reaction to a number of major corporate and accounting scandals, notably Enron and World-Com who had underreported line costs by *capitalizing* rather than *expensing*.

Stone walls and steel bars

SOX impacted many areas. One of them was hiring practices. Under SOX, company officers such as the CEO became *personally* liable for shareholder losses due to a lack of due diligence. In plain language that means a lack of doing their best to ensure that things are done correctly, up to par, responsibly, free of mishaps, etc. Simply put: SOX criminalized negligence. No longer could a CEO hide behind plausible deniability. No longer could a CEO say: "I was not aware that they were (or were not) doing that".

Hiring becomes a frightening and dangerous activity from this point of view. Every act of corporate negligence or malfeasance starts with a bad actor. CEOs needed to demonstrate clearly that they were making the very best efforts to ensure quality in this critical area of a company's operations.

Something that readers of a certain age know well, but that needs to be explained for younger generations, is that in olden days, *line managers* hired and fired. A line manager is something that scarcely exists today, for reasons that I am in the middle of explaining.

A line manager is a loose concept, basically a middle management executive with end-to-end responsibility for a department. Budget responsibility. Profit and loss if the department is revenue generating. People management: hiring, firing, mentoring, evaluating, approving time off, managing training and certification, expenses. Line managers had operating responsibility that required field experience and process expertise. They usually started as team members in the departments they managed. And because many of them had started at the bottom when they were young, they often did not have certifications and degrees. Just experience and judgment.

Here's the thing. If a CEO is going to rely on the experience and judgment of middle management in a post-SOX world, to avoid negligence she or he must make sure that here is some reliable system or process to verify that each and every middle manager has the *right kind* of experience and judgment.

There is however an easier, softer way: Outsource the burden of verification to a university or professional association. By making a degree or a certification (or even better, both!) the base criterion for all hires, the CEO can now claim due diligence. She or he can now say: "How could I have reasonably known that they were incompetent? They had a valid certification from a professional association" or "After four years at Harvard, I reasonably expected that we were hiring the best of the best".

To further distance the CEO from liability, one takes the majority of personnel decisions away from the (potentially undependable) line manager and gives them to a *human resources professional.* One certified by a professional association of course! Now the CEO has *two* layers of due diligence.

These days, before a hiring manager can even interview a single candidate, all undesirables (people without third-party accreditation) have been winnowed out by a SHRM-CP (Society for Human Resource Management Certified Professional)[3] who will not be tempted to overlook the all-important need for certification simply because the candidate happens to be exceptionally well-qualified for the job to be done.

Never mind that the SHRM-CP can hardly be expected to have the necessary expertise to properly assess if a programmer (or any other specialist candidate) is any good.

---

[3] Increasingly, this job is done by a computer, and the CV of a candidate who does not happen to possess the desired accreditation from the desired institutions will never even be seen by human eyes.

That is not the point. The mission is not to ensure that the very best, most qualified candidate gets the job. It is to eliminate all outliers, even if the outlier is on the exceptional end of the scale. The modern corporate HR recruiting department's true purpose is the modern equivalent of "nobody ever got fired for buying IBM". They control the incoming candidates to ensure that every hire is as inoffensive as possible, unlikely to disrupt the established order, and above all displays the right sort of "qualifications" on paper so that the hiring decision can be easily defended. Anyone in any way out of the ordinary is rejected before they can do any harm.

This is a recipe for mediocrity, a big part of the cause of IT project failure. However, I accept that it will not change. The recommendations I will make do not involve changing anything in this realm. As I keep saying: I do not expect what works for Google to work for the average public company.

I am describing and explaining, not complaining. I am explaining because it is difficult for anyone who entered the corporate workforce after 2002 to conceive of how different things were before that time, and because of that it is difficult to understand the problems created by corporate America's[4] response to SOX. Where someone from a later generation sees a simple fact of life, just the way things are, I see unintended negative consequences of well-meaning legislation.

SOX was a driving force in creating the modern *matrix managed* corporation where nobody is a single point of accountability, and decisions and risk are shared by a broad base of stakeholders. It is committee decision-making at the largest scale possible, and it is one of the reasons why tech "unicorns"[5] are among the very few daring and innovative forces in the US economy; a typical unicorn CEO does not know or care about all this red tape and governance.

They are very unlike a cautious and conservative Harvard MBA being groomed for an executive position at a consumer packaged-goods company; they're definitely not risk avoiders, cowering in fear at the possibility of an audit. They may be world-changers, wildcats, pleasing no one but themselves. And they are revitalizing the US economy. But to be fair, they are not burdened with legacy corporate

---

[4] And realistically: many corporations outside of the US.

[5] Private companies with valuations above US $1 billion.

culture and deep power structures that they can barely hope to control.

As I keep saying: I do not expect what works for a unicorn to work for the typical public corporation whose predicament I am addressing in this book. For better or for worse, we do live in a post-SOX world where responsibility is matrixed and the only excellence possible is excellence driven by process. In the last section of this book I will make my point about eliminating rampant project failure with recommendations on how to not only live with that reality, but to exploit it to reach levels of performance enjoyed by traditional manufacturing.

I'm Ed, I'll be your Project Manager

DILBERT © 2011 Scott Adams. Used By permission of ANDREWS MCMEEL SYNDICATION. All rights reserved.

But IT Portfolio Management and SOX were not the only culprits.

The second half of the first decade of the new millennium was a time when several driving forces converged to create "a perfect storm" in the area of corporate IT.

The focus on SOX compliance triggered intensified focus on IT. Swarms of auditors and risk analysts descended like locusts as the powerful finance executives decided that it was time for the "adults in the room" to take charge of the undisciplined savages and bring some order to the chaos factory. The collective trauma of IT managers only deepened, and they crawled ever deeper into the perceived safety of their cocoons of "no".

Meanwhile the PMI was at the top of their game. It rode in on a white horse and cast the project manager as the hero. Project Management Professionals (PMPs) with their certifications from a well-respected professional standards association fit the bill perfectly in a post-SOX world.

The project manager as hero was further aided by the matrix management trend. As dotted lines replaced solid lines on org charts, responsibility for results became diluted across numerous executives.

In many public companies today, there are multiple functional managers in IT; one for each area of expertise. There's a functional manager for the software architects, another one for the business analysts, and one for the developers, and one for the testers, and so on and so on.

Workers are assigned by these functional managers to a work under a project manager, who of course has his or her own functional manager. In a different organizational unit (usually), with a non-IT executive, there is the *program* manager whose responsibility is to make sure that a portfolio of projects for one business unit is completed on time and on budget. Usually there will also be a business solutions manager (reporting up to yet another operational business unit).

With responsibility everywhere and no-where, the certified project manager becomes king or queen, the one remaining person with clear end-to-end responsibility for a deliverable. The hero.

All the world's a stage

Finally, I am getting to the Stage-Gate.

Raising the project manager to hero status was not the only trick the PMI had up its sleeve. It also saw an opportunity to promote the Stage-Gate process, which it had been interested in for many years.

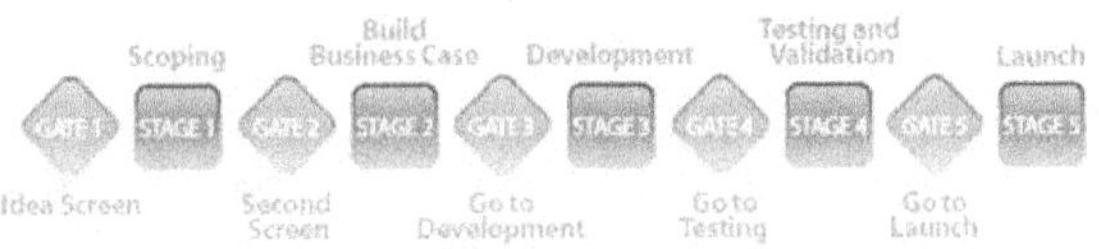

The concept is of a series of "gates" which are go-nogo decision points, following a phase or stage of activity which is then followed by another go-nogo gate.

It made all the bureaucrats very happy.

- Gates 1 and 2 pleased the proponents of IT Portfolio Management by providing a framework for checkpoints that supported its most fundamental goals of prioritization, and alignment with the corporate vision.
- Gate 3 served the needs of both IT Portfolio Management (Balanced investments across business units) and SOX (financial controls and auditable trails).
- Gate 4 facilitated compliance with SOP-98 by isolating the portions of a project that could be capitalized from the portions that could not.

CFOs greeted this process with relief and adopted it forthwith. In 2002, IT was still generally under the control (or at least strong influence) of Finance, and stage-gate became the standard way of managing IT projects. No questions asked. No questioning allowed.

In the years since then, corporate executives have turned a deaf ear to programmers and business analysts who have been urging their bosses to realize how destructive the whole system really is. Here is what they have been saying about the stage-gate process:

1) Stage-gate starts *budget battles* between business units. In most companies, budget for IT projects is not centrally allocated to and managed by IT (although I have seen this once). It usually comes from the business   units.

   Every division/department is out for itself and would rather have an eye poked out than use their budget for something that benefits all departments equally. The business aggressively pushes IT to make sure that every dollar of budget is spent in such a way that it benefits that department only.

   This leads to massive duplication at every

level from server infrastructure to application functionality.

2) The stage-gate project mentality forces integration to the *lowest common denominator*.

One of the most common customer complaints is: "Why can't they connect everything together? Why do I get 3 invoices instead of one, why can't I manage my mobile phone on the same page as my business line? Why do I have to make a phone call instead of doing it from my app?"

The source of these issues is a failure to integrate, which stems from the fact that that large interdependent applications are almost always broken up into small projects.

In order to pass audit, and be considered a "real" project, each one has to have a set of achievable goals that, once the work is completed, will stand on its own. Project managers' only incentives are to deliver the project on-time and on-budget. If you are a project manager, you are acutely aware that the more integrated your project is with other projects, the greater the risk that *someone else's* failure will cause *your* project to be over-budget or behind schedule.

As I explained earlier, accountability is scattered across a matrix organization at every level except for the project manager. Therefore, project managers enjoy almost absolute control over what happens inside the box of budget and schedule. Almost any violation of architectural guidelines or failure to integrate well with other projects will be tolerated by the organization because the project manager will get all of the latitude required to meet the budget and schedule constraints.

This leads project managers to ruthlessly drive integration down to the lowest possible common denominator; the less dependency there is between projects, the more disconnected they are, the more likely the project manager is to succeed.

3) The stage-gate approval process is *wasteful*.

As mentioned above, all but the smallest applications are broken up into multiple projects. Each project has to go through the stage-gate process in which a dossier is prepared and submitted to some sort of treasury approval before the project work starts. This approval is an essential step in a capital approval process that legitimizes the capitalization of development costs.

It is not unusual for the approvals process to consume between 30% and 50% of the project budget for smaller projects. If the approval process costs 50% of the budget, that means that the project costs twice as much as it needs to. The money is being spent on governance and preparation for a *possible* audit (the ever-present sword of Damocles that hangs over the project manager's head and inspires wide-eyed terror in IT managers).

IT could be accomplishing twice as much coding as it accomplishes today by putting governance on a diet. Since the governance clearly isn't working to prevent project failures, what purpose does it really serve?

4) The project mentality utterly destroys momentum and continuity.

As we said: all but the smallest applications are broken up into multiple projects and has to go through the stage-gate process.

In a happy fantasy world, these projects are approved one after another so that each phase proceeds smoothly from the last. In reality nothing could be farther from the truth. Budget freezes, poorly constructed dossiers, competition between projects, and many other factors conspire to practically guarantee that there will be large gaps of time between the projects that are supposed to be a seamless series of phases.

During these gaps, development teams must be disbanded. With no project budget to pay them, keeping them as a permanent team would *operationalize* them, creating operational expenses that lower profits.

When the team is disbanded valuable knowledge about the application is lost. No amount of documentation can make up for that. Even in the case of a perfectly documented project, the incoming team for the next "project" (actually just a phase in the development of one application) at least has to read the documentation, read the existing code, and get familiar and comfortable with it. Usually there is a lot of griping and complaining: "Why did they do *that*?" The reasons for things having been done a certain way are lost forever. Documentation only tells you the way things are, it almost never tells you *why*.

5) The stage-gate project mentality utterly destroys team dynamics and commitment.

The eternal churn, the reality that the person you are working with today will be gone tomorrow, the possibility that *you* will be gone tomorrow is utterly demoralizing.

At one of the large public corporations where I was a project manager the HR team stuck up some posters in the IT building. One of the posters came unstuck and fell to the floor. I watched as it lay on the floor for a week with people stepping over it or around it, or on it. This is a heart-rending illustration of the profound level of disengagement and disaffection pervading corporate IT.

It's my contention that the almost religious fervor with which Agile has been promoted by development teams is a direct reaction against the soul-destroying sense of futility that this type of project management culture has created. But as I said earlier, it has not worked, and there is no reason to believe that it will suddenly start working now.

One final irony

The Stage-Gate process is sometimes known as Phase-Gate, and also sometimes by another name, one that will be familiar to you by now: *the waterfall process*.

Yes, you read that correctly. In 2007, public companies were all working as hard as they possibly could to adopt the one process that all experts agreed was the wrong one. A process that had been discredited as far back as 1970.

It happened so gradually, that like the proverbial frog in slowly heated water, my colleagues who had remained in IT seemed only vaguely aware that they were being boiled alive.

However, I was coming back after having been away for a while. So, what I saw what was to me an abrupt regression from the progress and optimism of 2004 back to the befuddling quagmire of human misery and hopelessness that had inspired *The Mythical Man-Month* over three decades earlier.

"The beatings will continue until morale improves."

~ Anonymous

"No scene from prehistory is quite so vivid as that of the mortal struggles of great beasts in the tar pits...The fiercer the struggle, the more entangling the tar, and no beast is so strong or so skillful but that he ultimately sinks.

Large-system programming has over the past decade been such a tar pit, and many great and powerful beasts have thrashed violently in it. Most have emerged with running systems — few have met goals, schedules, and budgets. Large and small, massive or wiry, team after team has become entangled in the tar. No one thing seems to cause the difficulty — any particular paw can be pulled away. But the accumulation of simultaneous and interacting factors brings slower and slower motion. Everyone seems to have been surprised by the stickiness of the problem, and it is hard to discern the nature of it. But we must try to understand it if we are to solve it."

Frederick P. Brooks Jr.
The first two paragraphs of
The Mythical Man-Month

Chapter Nine
Aftermath

The last several years have seen phenomenal increases in programming productivity everywhere *except* in government and corporate IT.

In the late 50's and Sixties, compilers brought an order of magnitude improvement in coding productivity.

In the late 80's and early 90's, Class libraries added a few more orders of magnitude improvements.

Also, in the late 80's and early 90's, virtual machines with JIT (Just in Time) compilers reached maturity and added more again.

Now, open source code repositories have added a few more on to that, and in the last decade, there have appeared so many web services with free entry-level plans that a good programmer with a good idea can set up a proof of concept in days and build a whole business in weeks.

Start-ups and the big Internet giants have experienced a boom of epic proportions. The advent of massive repositories of free open source code have created an environment where not only do programmers stand on the shoulders of giants, but even the little guys are lifting each other up to the stratosphere.

However, enterprise IT in general has proven incapable of leveraging these same open source repositories and web-services to achieve anything like the lightning speed and quality user experience that even very large Internet companies are able to routinely access.

The reason for this is the same reason why less than a third of IT projects succeed. You will understand after I tell you some surprising things about industrialization.

Part Three

A brief overview of the evolution of manu-facturing, from the stone age to today. The dif-ference between Artisanal and Industrial manufacturing. What the history books don't teach.

"Man is a Tool-using Animal. Weak in himself, and of small stature, he stands on a basis, at most for the flattest-soled, of some half-square foot, insecurely enough; has to straddle out his legs, lest the very wind supplant him. Feeblest of bipeds! Three quintals are a crushing load for him; the steer of the meadow tosses him aloft, like a waste rag. Nevertheless he can use Tools, can devise Tools: with these the granite mountain melts into light dust before him; seas are his smooth highway, winds and fire his unwearying steeds. Nowhere do you find him without Tools; without Tools he is nothing, with Tools he is all."

Carlyle: "Sartor Resartus," Chap. IV.

Chapter Ten
Manufacturing: a 30-minute history

I am a big believer that there is always much to learn from looking at successful examples in other fields. In this case, there is much to learn about IT efficiencies and productivity from automobile manufacturing. But just as we did with programming, let's start at the very beginning. I believe you may learn some things that will truly surprise you.

Everything you think you know is wrong

For the bulk of human history, objects were made by hand. They were *manufactured*; *manu* being Latin for hand, *factus*, Latin for make.

Before I started to write this book, I thought I knew the difference between industrial and artisanal production. I thought the keys to modern industrialization were division of labor, assembly lines, factories, automation, and steam (later on: electrical) power.

Therefore, I was quite surprised to learn that there is evidence of division of labor — or *separation of concerns* to use the fancier sounding consultant's term — dating back to the stone age. There were specialists in chipping stone for spearheads and other specialists for creating axes, and they worked in separate areas[1].

Something else that may surprise you as it did me, is how far back in time humans were using assembly lines. Ancient bakeries produced bread in an assembly line fashion progressing from loading docks for raw materials to workstations that progressively transformed the raw materials into finished goods (bread)[2]. This, and other examples abound throughout history.

Factories also have a long history; the word itself, meaning a "building for making goods," first appeared in 1610.

Finally: automation is not so new. The ancients refined grains on a large scale with mills powered by animals (at first), or wind, water, and gravity (not long after) where foodstuff could be ground up between two stones.

---

[1] Bryson, B., 2004. *A Short History of Nearly Everything*, 1st ed. Broadway Books, New York. Churchill, S.E., Franciscus, R.G., McKean-Peraza, H.A., Daniel, J.A., Warren, B.R., 2009.

[2] Wilson, A.I., 2008a. Machines in Greek and Roman Technology, in: Oleson, J.P. (ed.), *e Oxford Handbook of Engineering and Technology in the Classical World*. Oxford University Press, Oxford, New York.

Similar types of automation were used for hammering (blacksmithing), pumping water, and sawing wood and stone or even keeping fires going with bellows.

The things my schoolbooks told me had brought about the industrial revolution were in fact old hat by the late 1800's. Specialization, assembly lines, factories, and automation had all been around for centuries, even millennia, before then.

Let me be clear: The Industrial Revolution was a profound societal upheaval, but it had little impact upon manufacturing productivity and quality.

To understand what really brought about the modern industrial age, I had to go back to fundamentals and look carefully to uncover *what changed* around the turn of the 20th century. What was there in 1950 that *was not there* in 1850, and when and where did it first appear? I learned that it all revolves around *skills*.

The Basics

How many of us could successfully create an effective spearhead by chipping at a piece of stone? There are secrets to the craft. *Craft* is the word we use to describe an activity that that requires particular skills and knowledge. Although different dictionaries have different definitions of the word, they *all* include the word *skill*.

Artisan is the word we use to describe people who practice a craft. A *master artisan* is a practitioner who has achieved the highest levels of skill. Mastery is the most important thing to understand about artisans and craftsmanship.

The words Master and Mastery are rich with connotations. In today's Western culture, some of those connotations are considered negative, but if we look at the origins of the word, it is quite benign. The Latin word *magister* meant as much *teacher* as it did *director*. It denotes authority, but that authority is derived from knowledge and ability, not fiat or force. A *tyrant* was the word for a ruler whose authority was imposed by force. A *master* was simply someone with a deep knowledge of something.

In manufacturing, mastery was very important. Back when *everything* was produced by hand, including raw materials, those materials were scarce and expensive. No one wanted to risk wasting them by putting them into the hands of anyone less than a master.

As I was writing this book, my editor asked me: "why do you refer to programming as a *craft*, when Knuth refers to it as an *art*?" I briefly answered the question by saying that art and craft are not mutually exclusive terms. You will find that all dictionaries also include the word skill somewhere in their definitions of *art*.

I do believe that there is a difference between art and craft. It is just that I do not think that any one domain must be exclusively one or the other. Music is not inherently more artistic than coding. I believe that art and craft are two interconnected aspects of any human pursuit. Craft is the body of knowledge that is passed from one practitioner to the next, sometimes lost and rediscovered, sometimes lost forever. It usually takes a long time to master a craft.

When mastery of a craft is accomplished, often it leads to a higher level of creativity. For example, I am a musician. I can tell you that to be able to improvise, I first needed to master the craft, starting with the basic functioning of my instrument (bass guitar). I needed to master the rules of western music (scales, intervals, chords), and I needed to have an extensive knowledge, if not a mastery, of the idiom or musical form in which I was playing (jazz). I had to listen to tens of thousands of hours of music to be able to construct a mental frame-work and understanding of what sounded good, and to groove it so deeply in my mind (and in my fingers) that I could make choices about what note to play next in 100th of a second. (Most music is played between 60 and 160 beats per minute.) I know it is the same for painters who must learn pigments, medium, canvas stretching, sizing, etc., and for sculptors and other kinds of artists.

I have met prodigies, who were creative immediately and seemed to have an instinctive grasp or mastery of the fundamentals of their art, but they are far and few between. For the vast majority, craft comes before artistry, and working through stages of learning towards mastery is a necessary prerequisite.

For thousands of years, *all* manufactured items were luxuries. Things you and I take for granted, such as shoes or clothes, were ex-tremely expensive and difficult to obtain espe-cially those made by the hand of a master shoe-maker or dressmaker. When you can only af-ford just one pair of shoes, or one dress, you want it to be the best it can be, and you want it to last as long as it can. Mastery was required to achieve this level of quality.

Reputation was also a factor. Not just an individual's reputation, but often the entire town in which he or she lived. Certain towns were known as centers of excellence for particular products, and a shoddy product could damage the reputation of an entire town. Reputation takes a long time to build, but only moments to destroy. There were many reasons why people were very concerned with who was a master artisan, and who was still learning.

We do not know much about how mastery was attained in pre-historic times (precisely because they are *pre*-historic), but enough archeological evidence remains from the latter part of what historians call *Classical Antiquity* to form a few theories.

Archeological studies of the remnants of pottery[3] from ancient India[4] and China[5] suggest that in the East, craft was mostly transmitted in a family setting, from parents to children, or by apprenticeship, which often included adopting someone into the family (Japan). Shortly thereafter, in the Roman Era, we also

---

[3] Pottery was one the main manufacturing activities of the times.

[4] Menon, J., & Varma, S. (2010). Children playing and learning: Crafting ceramics in ancient Indor Khera. *Asian Perspectives, 49*(1), 85–109.

[5] Barbieri-Low, A. J. (2007). *Artisans in early imperial China*. Seattle: University of Washington.

see the appearance of that Latin word *magister* used as a title denoting authority based upon expertise, and we see *collegae* (Latin for a group of colleagues or associates) now called collegium in English. Any group of colleagues was a collegium, even just a social club, but significantly, some of them were trade associations and legal entities. The biographer and historian Plutarch (46-120 A.D.) said that the Roman King Numa Pompilius classified the crafts into nine *collegia opificum:* flute players, goldsmiths, coppersmiths, carpenters, fullers, dyers, potters, shoemakers, and miscellaneous.

As I mentioned earlier, organization of factories and workshops, using both division of labor and production lines, was nothing new. It seems that humans have been doing this since pre-history. What was new in the Roman Era was the emergence of *social* organization. The *collegia opificum* marked the beginnings of the professional trade associations that were not entirely family based.

Trade associations were to have a profound influence on the evolution of manufacturing (and in fact on society at large). By the High Middle Ages in the 12th century, we start to see evidence of a formal system for trade associations emerging in what is now Europe. That system was what we know as the *guild* system. (The guilds had many names for themselves at the time.)

The rise and fall of guilds took place over 700 years. Its peak was during the two-hundred years that followed the Black Death when guilds dominated civic life. During those two centuries, guild membership was as critical as Communist Party membership was in Soviet Russia or Maoist China, with the larger more influential guilds controlling just about every aspect of local politics, and even having influence at a national and international level.

The journey to mastery

The guilds controlled the career progression of their artisan members with an iron fist, and they acknowledged three distinct stages in an artisan's professional life. The first stage was apprentice. In the earlier centuries of the guild system it was common for apprentices to be *adopted* by the master artisans they were apprenticed to. It supports the theory that transmission of craft knowledge was seen as something to be kept in the family. The apprentice's family would pay the master to adopt the apprentice at an early age because it was the only way to enter a guild and being a guild member was one of the most secure positions anyone could hope for in those times.

Usually the apprentice was *indentured* and forgive me for taking a little side-trip to talk about indenture. The word is just fabulous and reveals so much about human ingenuity. An *indenture* was a form of contract, usually one where a human was placed in servitude. The contract would be written in duplicate side by side on the same sheet of paper. To guarantee authenticity the duplicates would then be separated from each other by tearing or cutting in an irregular pattern so that each would match up only with the original other half.

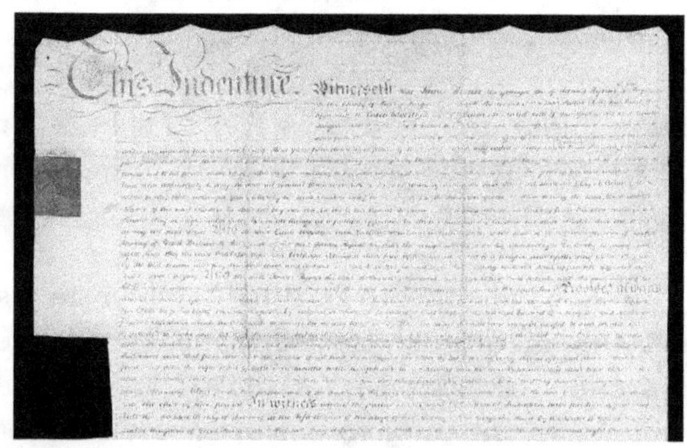

The Norman word for teeth is *dent*. The irregular separation of the contract was like teeth, therefore in-*dent*-ure.

Apprentices started with the most menial of tasks: sweeping, fetching, washing, and the like. They were permitted only to observe the master and the other workers and learn by watching. Slowly, progressively, over years, apprentices would be given access to tools and materials, being tested every step of the way. For hundreds of years, the period of apprenticeship varied from guild to guild, from master to master, but in 1563 England passed the Statute of Artificers and Apprentices[6] which set a 7-year minimum period for all apprenticeships. This gives us a good idea of what might have been considered a normal or typical apprenticeship period in the previous centuries.

By the early 15th century we see the word *journeyman* appearing in historical documents. Once apprentices graduated, they were no longer indentured and were free to charge for their labor by the day; *Journée* is French for day.

Journeymen were certified by their guilds as having all of the basic skills and knowledge to produce the articles of their trade. Some would never attempt to become masters, preferring the freedom to come and go as they pleased. Those who wanted to become masters would work for several more years

---

[6] "Research, education & online exhibitions > Family history > In depth guide to family history > People at work > Apprentices". **The** National Archives. Archived from the original on 27 July 2008. Retrieved 2008-06-16.

accumulating skill and experience before petitioning the guild to admit them as masters.

Different guilds placed different demands upon petitioners. Sometimes the guild would want to limit the number of masters in a particular field or location to prevent too much competition. But there was always the question of skill. Many guilds demanded that the applicants create a piece of work that demonstrated mastery. That's where the word *masterpiece* comes from.

The guilded cage

The guild system was designed to protect the reputation (and profitability) of the crafts by ensuring mastery, but it had weaknesses that stemmed from everything being arranged for the convenience of the masters.

The system tended to discourage innovation. Masters did not want apprentices or journeymen outshining them. They also felt that a certain type of product was the guild's *brand* and deviating from what were essentially brand guidelines was usually sternly disapproved of.

It was chaotic. When one reads the history, one thing comes up over and over again:

Workers, especially masters, did *as they pleased*. Even in factory environments. This, or some very similar turn of phrase, is repeated constantly in the literature. It is very clear that there were no objective standards. Methods, results, and professional behavior were up to individual guilds, and often simply up to individuals. Even factory workers would routinely spend up to half their time in business for themselves, using factory space and materials to do so.

Most importantly: these industries did not scale. This was partly by design; masters deliberately limited their number to prevent supply from exceeding demand. The guild system ensured there were never quite enough master artisans to produce enough goods for everyone.

This is quite anti-democratic[7] when you think about it. Consumers were being deliberately denied access to affordable necessities, such as clothing, shoes, and farming tools, so that an artisanal elite could keep prices high. Prior to the Industrial Revolution, most people had to make *everything* themselves unless they could pay someone else to do it. They wore shoes they carved out of wood themselves.

---

[7] Democracy as the practice or principles of social equality, not as a political system.

They wore clothes they made themselves (perhaps after a 15-hour day of working in the fields). Basic items like knives or tables and chairs were prized heirlooms that were preciously handed down from generation to the next.

The weakness of a society whose economy is based on artisanal production, is that it's fundamentally inequitable. Only the wealthiest individuals can afford artisanal products. Industrial production has made everyday items attainable for everyday people. I believe that it is no accident that the more democratic the country, the more rapidly and enthusiastically it adopted industrial production methods to its advantage.

Tackling the problem of blocks

The Venetian Arsenal will be my starting point to describe the beginning of the end of artisanal production. Originally built in the 12th Century its fortunes almost perfectly paralleled that of the guilds that provided the workforce to this naval factory[8]. It rose to its peak at about the same time as the guilds, and its decline and destruction came just at the

---

[8] Another surprise to me: factories were not an invention of the Industrial Revolution, they predate that by quite a while.

beginning of the Industrial revolution, as the guilds were declining.

It was a factory for producing ships. The big wooden kind with sails. Some people feel it was the first factory, others dispute this, and it really comes down to what your definition of factory is. What nobody disputes however is that at its peak in the 1600's, it was the largest manufacturing site in Europe with as many as sixteen-thousand[9] workers toiling to produce ships for the Venetian navy.

To name a few of the many types of craftsmen and craftswomen: shipwrights (a dozen types), caulkers, oar makers, mast makers, pulley makers, wood carvers, cask makers, gun carriage makers, rope makers, cannon casters, stevedores, blacksmiths, sawyers, framers, bakers, fitters and many others.

I will single out the pulley makers because theirs would be the first jobs in history to become truly industrialized, although not at the Arsenal, where the guilds held sway until the very end (which would come in 1796), but rather at Royal Navy Dockyards in Portsmouth.

---

[9] Wikipedia and other popular sources frequently cite this number, however some of the more scholarly sources I have read in my research put the number much lower, in one case as low as three thousand.

The pulleys used on a ship are called *blocks*, as in *block and tackle*. Blocks were vitally important to navies. You build a ship once. It wears out very slowly. Blocks are moving parts that bear heavy loads. They are used to load supplies and to tighten rigging, which creates a lot of wear and tear, and they need to be replaced often. In the 1700's the British Navy alone consumed about one-hundred thousand blocks a year. They were what we would now call *mission critical.* That is to say: a crucial component essential to the functioning of a business. It is no exaggeration to say that without blocks, there would have been no navies.

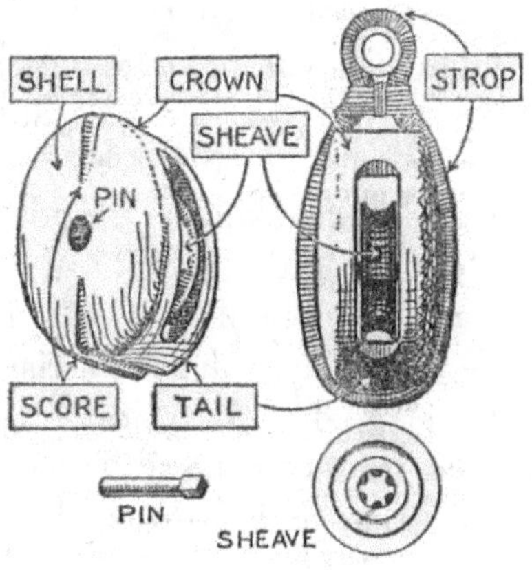

Parts of a block (Seaman's Pocket-Book, 1943)

Samuel Bentham, a talented shipwright and naval architect, found his first employment with Prince Potemkin of Russia in 1780. His talent was recognized early, and Bentham was given great responsibility and great freedom to experiment. In 1787, Bentham took charge of the "grossly mismanaged factories" in southern Russia where there was such a lack of skilled artisans that he felt he had no alternative other than to set to work "on the problem of *'transferring skill'* by means of machines, so that *unskilled workmen* might be made to produce the same results as skilled labor"[10] (italics mine). He was rewarded by Potemkin with a knighthood and was made a brigadier general.

This question of transferring skill is central to the argument I will make in Part 3. This is because there are two kinds of automation. One can automate a repetitive task that requires no particular skill. My food processor automates chopping things up, but it does not do so with any appreciable level of skill. Things are chopped up willy-nilly. An artisanal sushi chef would be appalled. In the other type of automation, one transfers the skill of master to a machine. My rice cooker does a better job at

---

[10] Roe, Joseph Wickham. *English And American Tool Builders*. 2nd ed., London, McGraw-Hill Book Company, Inc., 1926,23. Most of the information on this page and the next are from this source.

cooking rice—perfectly—than I ever will be able to do on a stovetop with a saucepan. Even master sushi chefs use rice machines.

Skill is at the heart of manufacture. Automating with brute force helps a bit but it does not provide a quantum leap in productivity. Automating skills does.

For the rest of this book, I am going to use the word robot for machines that have had skill transferred to them. My rice cooker is a robot. My food processor is not.

Upon Potemkin's death in 1791, Bentham returned to Britain, and promptly took out patents on the robots that he conceived of while in Russia. As a senior naval officer of an allied country (Russia and England were allied against France during the French Revolutionary Wars), his ideas gained an audience with the British Admiralty who were impressed enough to create the office of Inspector General in 1796 so that Bentham would have the authority to put his recommendations into effect.

The Portsmouth Royal Dockyard was founded in 1650, and by 1796 was the most important facility in the British Navy. Bentham (who had served his seven-year apprenticeship at Portsmouth) turned his attention to the ship-building there. The Venetian Arsenal had been looted and shut down when the French annexed Venice and Portsmouth was now the largest manufacturing complex in the world. Under Bentham's tutelage, it also became the site of the first *industrialization* in the world.

I must pause the narrative here to make something clear: I use the word *industrialization* in a very particular manner. Although I do not believe that any scholar would contest my definition as being totally incorrect, I am sure that many — if not most — would protest that it is incomplete and too narrow.

Fine. I am not attempting to write a comprehensive history of either manufacturing or of industrialization, and I am not an historian. My goal is to sensitize the reader to two key aspects of industrialization that no serious scholar could dispute are essential. They are *transfer of skill to machinery* and *producing interchangeable parts*.

I will completely ignore two other aspects that are the first two things most people (including historians) think of when speaking of industrialization: *division of labor* and *assembly lines*. Why? Because as I demonstrated at the start of the chapter, those two things have been around as far back as history and archeology allow us to go. They were around for a long time before anything that could possibly be called industrialization. So, I am forced to conclude that although they may be things that are present in industrialization, they cannot be considered the *cause* of it.

When I say that that Portsmouth was the birthplace of industrialization, it is because Bentham's work there was the first historically documented case of robots producing interchangeable parts, implemented at scale, in a long-running production process (his robots remained in use until 1965).

As I told you I looked for *what changed*, and this is what I found. Robots and interchangeable parts are the two innovations that *actually* brought about industrialization and the modern age we live in.

At Portsmouth, Bentham installed steam powered belt drives that powered automated devices such as pumps and saws, but he paid especially close attention to block-making as lending itself well to his ideas for robotic automation. His vision was twofold when he set about designing the machinery. First, that it could be operated by *unskilled* laborers, and second that it would produce blocks of a *better quality* than most artisans could make.

Quality was as important as quantity and cost. The overall quality of the artisanally manufactured blocks was spotty. Some of the blocks were just terrific, the best blocks, beautiful blocks. However, there were just as many inferior blocks that would break under load or snag or catch fire because of friction. At the best of times, nobody much likes fire on a boat, but in combat, or in heavy seas, these failures could be fatal.

Bentham's machines were made so that unskilled laborers would fasten rough blocks of wood to the machine, and then start it by pulling a lever connecting it to the overhead belt-driven power source. The machine would then shape the block and cut the slots with a very high degree of consistency. The parts were close to perfect every time and could therefore be assembled with no *fitting*.

The significance of this last part was largely overlooked by his contemporaries, who focused their efforts to improve efficiency on division of labor and the economies of scale obtained from having everyone in the same factory as opposed to scattered about in cottage workshops (as previously had been the case).

The inventors Henry Maudslay and Marc Isambard Brunel (father of Isambard Kingdom Brunel, who is generally recognized as one of the great figures of the Industrial Revolution) joined Bentham's team. The block shaping machine above was one of the fruits of their collaboration, it carved ten blocks at time.

The result was faster, better, and cheaper. Ten unskilled laborers did the work that previously took one-hundred and ten skilled (and expensive) guild members. But more importantly: The new blocks were better. They had less friction, broke less often, snagged lines less, and overall had a much longer life than the old blocks[11].

---

[11] Cooper, C.C., 1984. e Portsmouth System of Manufacture. *Technology and Culture* 25, 182–225. doi:10.2307/3104712.

It is said no good deed goes unpunished; Bentham was no exception. His improvements to the system were disruptive. Some of the inefficiencies he removed were graft and corruption that had been quite favorable for certain members of the Admiralty, and Bentham found himself progressively squeezed out over a seven-year period. However, some of the ideas and work of Bentham, Maudslay, and the Brunels (both Marc and Isambard Kingdom), spread throughout England and Europe. As a result, the Industrial Revolution started in the late 1700s. By sometime between 1820 and 1840, England and Europe had almost completely overthrown the guild system in favor of the *factory system*.

Many historians miss the significance of robots and interchangeable parts. They tend to focus on textile production, the introduction of steam power, and the raised standard of living. However, the lynchpin of the Industrial Revolution was the factory system which at its best was typified by the use of unskilled labor made possible by methods and economies of scale first demonstrated at Portsmouth.

Clone wars

Before I go on with the story, I want to do my best to impress upon you how completely differently you think about objects in the world than people did for almost all of human history.

You take it completely for granted that the products you buy and use are, for all practical purposes, identical with all of the other products of that brand and model. If you were a classic car buff, and had a 1973 Chevrolet Caprice Classic convertible, you could buy a second or third car of the same year and model just to use for spare parts. You would be shocked and disbelieving if your local garage mechanic told you that he could not use a wheel, or a seat, or an engine from the parts car without extensive machining and custom work to make it fit. You expect it to bolt right in and work right away.

The same is true for every device or object in your life. You expect every iPhone case to fit your iPhone the same way it fits your friend's iPhone. You expect that if you had a matched dining room set, that you could take the legs from a chair with a broken seat and put them on a chair with broken legs.

If your TV dies, you expect that you can go out and buy a new one that uses the same wall mount as the old one and plugs into all of the same satellite receivers and DVD players as the old one, using the same cables.

You expect that there is an unlimited supply of parts for everything you own, and you expect that those parts can be replaced in minutes or, at most, in hours.

You live in a world where uniformity and regularity are taken for granted. What you likely do not know, and never think about, is that over humanity's ten-thousand-year existence this uniformity is a very recent experience. It started just two hundred years ago, and it didn't really become commonplace until after World War Two.

Even *after* the Industrial Revolution, *nothing* in the world was uniform or regular. This is important: The Industrial Revolution did *not include standardization*. At the end of the period that historians call the Industrial Revolution, *every* factory, *every* machine in every factory, *every* process, and *every* single product created was *utterly and entirely unique*.

Furthermore, if you would have been so bold as to suggest to someone that it was possible to make identical things with identical machines and create products that were for all practical purposes identical, you would have been dismissed as a dangerous lunatic. The philosophy of artisanal production with each master's idiosyncratic approach as an ineluctable fact of life was deeply ingrained from thousands of years of practice. The very idea of identical products was as heretical a thought as the idea of a spherical earth, or a solar system with the sun at the center, once were. It was—to use the favorite expression of Vizzini in *The Princess Bride*—inconceivable!

As difficult as it is for the modern reader to imagine, there were armies of workers whose only tool was a file. Their job: to file away until two parts fit together. No product, not a single table, chair, or pair of shoes, could be made without passing through the hands of several fitters who existed solely to *adjust* what had already been made.

Friends in high places

It was in the area of firearms manufacture where fitting was finally eliminated.

Firearms originated during the High Middle Ages in China where gunpowder was first discovered just as the guilds were emerging in England and Europe. For seven hundred years firearms would be manufactured using artisanal production methods, with master gunsmiths producing each firearm individually.

As armies grew bigger, and dependence upon firearms grew greater, demand increased dramatically. During the Industrial Revolution much effort was made to apply new techniques to musket manufacture, however the Industrial Revolution's "bag of tricks" simply could not be made to work for the production of muskets.

This was because the metal parts of a gun simply could not tolerate the same lack of precision that other common products of the Industrial Revolution could. It did not matter much if a few warps of a weave were not perfectly parallel, or if a pulley block was $1/100^{th}$ of inch wider at the top than at the bottom. But make a $1/100^{th}$ of an inch mistake on certain parts of a gun, and you could kill or maim the shooter. This is not good for business. Therefore, muskets continued to be manufactured exclusively by using the traditional methods of casting, forging, and carving the parts before giving them to master gunsmiths who would then *fit* them together meticulously.

Fitting consisted of filing a part, checking it with a *gage* (the historical predecessor to modern gauges) which was a piece of metal with notches cut in it, and filing again until the parts fit neatly with no play. Fitting and filing were taken so much for granted that nobody thought there was anything unusual or inefficient in taking a 2-kilogram block of metal and filing away 90% of the material to make a 200-gram trigger guard[12]. An armory would have hundreds of thousands of files in stock and would wear out approximately one file per gun.

As late as 1915, the records for the British Ministry of Munitions indicate that out of the twenty-five job titles involved in the manufacture of guns, six of them had the word fitter or filer in them[13].

At the beginning of the Industrial Revolution, French gunsmith Honoré Blanc tried valiantly to convince his countrymen of the importance of interchangeable parts for musket manufacture. In spite of dedicating his entire career to this end, he made no headway. For the most part, his compatriots simply weren't interested. He died in 1801 without ever having succeeded in promoting his inventions.

But his cause would continue to be championed for decades. His patron in the French

---

[12] Gordon, R.B., 1988. *Material Evidence of the Manufacturing Methods Used in "Armory Practice."* IA. *e Journal of the Society for Industrial Archeology* 14, 23–35.

[13] Great Britain. Ministry of Munitions *Official history of the Ministry of Munitions. Volume IV, The supply and control of labour 1915-16.* Andrews UK, Luton, 2012,90.

Army, General Jean-Baptiste de Gribeauval was a true believer in the importance of interchangeable parts and had many loyal subordinates who carried on his belief after his death in 1789. One of them, Major Louis de Tousard, escaped the French Revolution by emigrating to the United States, where he joined the V.S. Corps of Artillerists and Engineers. He was tremendously influential. Future military leaders served under him and adopted his beliefs. He is credited with having created the "blueprint" for West Point, and his book the American *Artillersit's Companion* etched his mentor Gribeauval's ideas indelibly on the minds of the American military[14].

Thomas Jefferson was another convert, having witnessed demonstrations of Blanc's achievements while serving as the Minister to France for the United States of America. For the next 25 years, Jefferson would pass through the offices of Secretary of State, Vice-President, and then finally President of the United States of America. The true believers in interchangeable parts had a powerful ally.

---

[14] Hounshell, David A. (1984), *From the American System to Mass Production, 1800-1932: The Development of Manufacturing Technology in the United States*, Baltimore, Maryland: Johns Hopkins University Press, ISBN 978-0-8018-2975-8, LCCN 83016269

It is hard to say what life today would be like if it had not been for this small group of powerful men who believed so strongly in something that was dismissed and ridiculed by the vast majority of society and the ruling elite. They took huge political risks, spent millions of dollars, and endured for decades in their pursuit of a goal that "reasonable" men dismissed as fantasy. It was not easy to achieve, but when they finally succeeded, it would change the face of the entire world forever.

Curve-jumping, paradigm-shifting cowboys:
The American system of manufacture

There is a curious gap in conventional Western history. Historians agree that from 1760 to 1830 was the era named *The Industrial Revolution*. The period from 1880 to 1940 is sometimes termed *The Machine Age*, while other historians call that period *the Technological Revolution*.

What happened in the fifty intervening years? There is no name for it in the history books, but something happened all right. In 1830 the United States of America was a backwater colony so small and insignificant that its first bank robbery was still a year away. Sixty years later, it was an industrial world power. How did this happen?

In 1777, the United States had just won its independence from Britain in a war that lasted eight long years; a war won by the Americans with cannons and muskets, lots of muskets. Many of these muskets were British muskets, muskets made by the very nation against which they were fighting. The rest had been purchased at great cost from France.

The new country decided that controlling its own arms manufacture would be essential to ensuring continued independence, and thus it established two national armories: Springfield and Harper's Ferry. The goings on at Springfield have been extensively researched by both historians, and *industrial archeologists*[15].

These unaccounted-for years saw five decades of sustained effort at the Springfield and Harper's Ferry armories to achieve interchangeable parts. This effort led to the invention of many new machine tools, and in collaboration with private companies, the American armories succeeded in producing muskets that

---

[15] It turns out that there are scholars who dig up bits of machinery and things made by machine and examine them with microscopes to determine if they were made by hand or by machine, and what kind of machine made them in which year. *Who knew?*

were so uniform, so regular, that in 1853 a visiting inspector from England was able to randomly select ten muskets made in ten different years, disassemble them, mix up the parts, and re-assemble ten functional muskets using only a screwdriver[16].

The impossible had been achieved: parts had been manufactured to such tight tolerances (a thousandth of an inch) that anyone could perform the assembly in a few minutes. Musket assembly no longer required years of skill and experience.

The way this was achieved was by building robots, and then using parts built by those robots to build *other better* robots, and then using the improved parts made by the better robots to build *even more advanced* robots that could finally meet the thousandth of an inch tolerance.

Transfer of skill to machines makes it possible to manufacture interchangeable parts of consistently high quality and consistent dimensions. The high quality and uniformity of those parts make it possible to build better machines, and so on. It is a virtuous circle.

------

[16] (Hounshell *ibid*)

As it happened, the Springfield Armory made extensive use of private contractors. These contractors would then spread the techniques throughout the United States, and this was the foundation for the *Technological Revolution* and the American domination of the *Machine Age*.

The levels of safety, reliability, and *affordability* of goods that we enjoy today would not be possible in an artisanal system of manufacture even though artisanal production could give us the first two. NASA space vehicles are a good example of safety and reliability produced by a highly artisanal process. They are also famous for their high costs and limited quantities.

Producing very large quantities at affordable prices is simply not possible without industrialized interchangeable parts and transfer of skill to machines.

At the beginning of Part Two, I said that I believe you will learn some things that might truly surprise you. In summary, here they are:

1. The Industrial Revolution did not completely automate production of everyday goods.

Well after the Industrial Revolution, significant manual labor was still required to fit pieces together. For the first 5 years of production, Ford still depended entirely on fitters to file down parts to join properly together.

2. Assembly lines and division of labor are not what makes production "industrialized".

Assembly lines and division of labor have existed since earliest recorded history. What *really* makes production industrialized is transfer of skill from human to machine and completely interchangeable parts which require no fitting.

3. Industrialization is quite possibly more morally virtuous than artisanal production.

Artisanal production is elitist both in terms of who can obtain gainful employment, and who can afford to purchase manufactured goods. Industrialization is inherently more democratic. Compared to agrarian and artisanal economies industrialization has undeniably raised the standard of living for huge numbers of people throughout history due to higher wages and better access to manufactured goods. Modern society may have many ills, but none of them would be cured by returning to an elitist artisanal manufacturing model.

4. Industrially made products can be higher-quality than hand-made products.

Industrial production does not mean sacrificing quality or luxury. Industrially made products often surpass the quality of hand-made products by every measure. The 1950's Mercedes 220 S pictured below is a beautiful piece of hand craftsmanship, but the Vision Mercedes-Maybach 6 Cabriolet just as beautiful, and infinitely safer and more reliable.

1950's Mercedes 220S

Vision Mercedes-Maybach 6 Cabriolet

At the lower end of the automotive scale, a Nissan Micra is *more* attractive and luxurious than a Model T in every possible way, as well as being more reliable.

Modern mass-produced violins have outperformed Stradivari in blind testing, and the most popular electric guitars in the world (the Fender Stratocaster) have always been mass-produced using interchangeable parts. Famous guitar players have cited the consistency of quality as their main reason for preferring them.

We have every reason to want to industrialize IT, and in the next chapter I will describe how to do it.

Chapter Eleven
Modern automobile manufacture

The last thing I would like to do before returning to the subject of programming and IT projects is to tell you about how cars are manufactured. This will help explain and justify my solutions for IT.

Automobile production is perhaps the most highly automated and industrialized sector in the world. In its 2017 executive summary of world robotics, the International Federation of Robotics informs us that 35% of the world's industrial robots are used in the automotive industry which puts it ahead of even the semiconductor and electronics industries.

This industrialization has paid off handsomely. Modern cars are better every year in every way you can measure. They are safer, more reliable, more luxurious, get better gas mileage and last longer with every passing year. But only a few decades ago, cars were as unreliable as software is today.

Enterprise IT would be doing well indeed if it could reach the same levels of quality and affordability as the auto industry. With that in mind, let's see how the motor vehicle industry does it.

Requirement

Every modern car model starts as a market need. Before anything else, the manufacturer decides *who* the car is intended for, and *why* they need a car. Is it for hauling children or construction materials? Or for status, or for fun?

Design

For about a year engineers and designers work together to create the new model. It is a painful and difficult process. It is a process of unhappy compromises. Every new car starts off as a list of budgets. The car cannot cost more than X. It cannot consume more than Y miles per gallon. The electrical accessories cannot drain more Z current from the battery. There is even a budget for air! Only so much air can be scooped up by the front grill. The engine designers want it to feed the carburetor, the brake designers want it to cool the brakes. The HVAC engineers want it for the cabin. And those are just a few of the people fighting for air.

Designers create designs that executives fall in love with only to be told that the sheet metal cannot be twisted that way, or it would make the car too heavy, slow, or hungry for gas.

Engineers use CAD models on computers and designers use sketch pads, charcoal, and clay models to create several designs, and after much back and forth, and seemingly infinite changes and re-adjustments because of those changes, a single design is selected from the candidates and the prototyping starts.

Test and debugging

Over the next year or two actual working prototype cars are built by hand by hand. Hundreds of cars will be cobbled together this way before the first mass produced car ever sees the light of day.

Several things are taking place during this time: Engineers are testing the design, to see if it works in real life. Parts are being tested to see if there are any unexpected interactions between any of the 10,000+ parts on the car (more about that later). Other engineers are figuring out how the car-building robots and sheet metal stamping molds need to be configured to be able to mass produce the car.

Production

The job is just starting. Every detail of the preceding steps (except possibly the requirements) will be revisited, refined, and re-done over and over again as production reveals defects that need to be corrected at the source of the problem.

Toyota, the company whose Toyota Production System inspired the just-in-time and lean manufacturing practices, as well as having inspired some of the Agile and DevOps approaches in IT, is being careful to keep a human involvement in the production line. Humans are better at improvement and innovation than machines (for now, and I believe forever), and Toyota does not want to fall behind in that regard.

By avoiding total automation and maintaining human involvement in every aspect of the production line, they ensure the continual improvement that will keep them competitive and make this year's cars better than last year's.

And that is why cars are so reliable today, a dramatic contrast to the many under-par IT projects today.

Part Four

Application development is an artisanal process and it is breaking under the strain of the current scale and growth.

How to "do it right." Modern automobile manufacturing is an example of how design and tooling do not need to be industrialized, only production.

"How can we make sure we wind up behind the right door when the going gets
tough? The answer is: craftsmanship."

~ Robert C. Martin,
Clean Code: A Handbook of
Agile Software Craftsmanship

Chapter Twelve
Modern day artisans

It is shocking to think that two hundred years after the industrial revolution, the one industry that is considered to be the most modern of our modern era is still completely and utterly artisanal.

But there it is. I put it to you as an undeniable fact that successfully creating an enterprise scale software application depends entirely upon being able to secure one or more master programmers, who will assume end to end responsibility, and who will mentor and guide novice and journeymen programmers in the application of their *craft*.

If you feel yourself rejecting this idea, ask yourself the opposite: could anyone could reasonably expect a complex software project to be successfully completed on time and on budget with a team composed entirely of *inexperienced* and/or *unskilled* programmers?

Now consider this: we *fully expect* that the apparatus that our lives depend upon, cars, airplanes, and medical devices, be correctly and safely built by teams of unskilled and semi-skilled workers (who, because of turnover, are also often inexperienced) who are only able to perform one small part of the process and would never be able to build a whole car, airplane, or medical device all by themselves. Of course, by now, we know how this works: transfer of skill to machinery and interchangeable mass-produced components.

Software application development is stuck at the place where auto manufacturing was before Ford introduced the Model T.

Guilded cage (redux)

Many of the people I wrote about in Parts One and Two have continued to contribute to and influence the field of programming, perhaps none more so than Robert C. Martin, professionally known as Uncle Bob. You might remember he encouraged the creation of Agile Manifesto.

Of all of the people who met there in Utah at the Snowbird ski resort in 2001, Uncle Bob is among the most visible and active today. He writes and speaks publicly about *craftsmanship*, professional ethics, code quality, and gender equality in programming. There are many videos of his talks on YouTube. As I write this, his most recent book is in the Amazon top 500 bestsellers *across all categories of books*. Pretty amazing for a book about programming written by a programmer for programmers. A lot of people agree with what he has to say. He invites us to consider the following:

He estimates (informally) that the number of programmers in the world doubles every five years or so. Which means, by definition, that at any moment in time, half the programmers in the world have less than five years of experience, which "leaves our industry in a state of perpetual inexperience".[1]

When the flood of new programmers entered the market in the late Seventies and early Eighties many of them were self-taught, unmentored, learning by example. Exponential growth every decade, ever-increasing workloads, and just-get-it-done culture has created generations of programmers doomed to "repeat the mistakes of everyone else over and over".

Uncle Bob makes it clear through the body of his work, that he believes that it is essential to create something resembling a guild by establishing programming as a *profession* with standards, ethics, accepted practices, and practices that are condemned and rejected.

---

[1] https://youtu.be/ecIWPzGEbFc at 51 minutes.

An important unspoken implication is that the current artisanal system is disorganized and chaotic. As you can see from the title of the book, I definitely feel this is the case.

And I generally agree with Uncle Bob because even though I am not a particularly good programmer myself, I love programming, and want it to flourish and thrive and perhaps more than anything, I sincerely want to improve the lives of millions of people laboring in the "salt mines" of modern IT, condemned to a cycle of fear, then failure, then recrimination, just so that they can bring home a paycheck and put food on the table.

The three reasons why I qualify this with "*generally* agree" are:

I suspect that parts of his vision may be too western-centric. For example, his exhortations for professional ethics, that programmers should flat out refuse to write unethical programs (such as the Volkswagen "diesel cheat"), might be much easier for programmers in Germany or the U.S. than for programmers in India or China.

Next, professional associations – like all human institutions – tend to accumulate cruft[2]. We see things like self-perpetuating bureaucracies, uncontrolled "organic" proliferation of rules or standards, and over-complexification of something that started off very simply. Uncle Bob himself feels that some of these things have already happened to Scrum/Agile.

Finally, guilds, unions, and other associations, have an unfortunate history of suppressing innovation in the name of "being fair to everyone".

Apart from these reservations I agree with everything Uncle Bob has to say… but regretfully; I do not believe that "professionalizing" programming will have a major impact upon the rate of IT project failure. Instituting a guild system of some sort will not provide the kind of scalability that the world is demanding, however I still think it is a good idea.

How can this be? How do I reconcile this with my proposal to industrialize IT, which we now know means using workers unskilled in programming? I will answer that question in the last chapter of this part and the first chapter of Part Four.

---

[2] *See Jargon File*

"Most software today is very much like
an Egyptian pyramid with millions of
bricks piled on top of each other, with
no structural integrity, but just done by
brute force and thousands of slaves."[3]

~ Alan Kay

[3] Stuart Feldman. 2004. A Conversation with Alan Kay. *Queue* 2, 9 (December 2004), 20-30. DOI: http://dx.doi.org/10.1145/1039511.1039523

Chapter Thirteen
No New Ideas

"IT industrialization is the next great phase in information technology."

— Al Zollar
GM of IBM Tivoli 1977 to 2011

Nothing new under the sun

As I stated at the start of the book: I propose the industrialization of IT and application development. Now, I expect that at least some of you are asking: if this is such a great idea, how come nobody has thought of it before?

The answer is of course, it *has* been thought of – and tried – many times before, by some very smart people. I have already written about some of those efforts, and I will introduce you to some new ones in this chapter.

I'll start with this Wikipedia entry[1]:

"Ad hoc code reuse has been practiced from the earliest days of programming. Programmers have always reused sections of code, templates, functions, and procedures.

---

[1] https://en.wikipedia.org/wiki/Code_reuse

Software reuse as a recognized area of study in software engineering, however, dates only from 1968 when Douglas McIlroy of Bell Laboratories proposed basing the software industry on reusable components."

McIlroy made his proposal for "Mass Produced Software Components" at a conference sponsored by the NATO Science Committee held in Garmisch, Germany, the 7th to 11th October 1968.

He opened his paper with this:

"We undoubtedly produce software by backward techniques… Software production today appears in the scale of industrialization somewhere below the more backward construction industries. I think its proper place is considerably higher, and would like to investigate the prospects for mass-production techniques in software."

He added:

"Of course mass production, in the sense of limitless replication of a prototype, is trivial for software. But certain ideas from industrial technique I claim are relevant...The idea of interchangeable parts corresponds roughly to our term 'modularity,' and is fitfully respected. The idea of machine tools has an analogue in assembly programs and compilers. Yet this fragile analogy is belied when we seek for analogues of other tangible symbols of mass production. There do not

exist manufacturers of standard parts, much
less catalogues of standard parts. One may
not order parts to individual specifications
of size, ruggedness, speed, capacity, precision or character set."

McIlroy was well ahead of his time. His
paper did not trigger immediate industry action, so he went on to quietly lead the Unix
team, and to create Unix *pipes*, the part of Unix
that makes it possible to connect small programs together. As I explained in Chapter Two
there is an underlying philosophy to Unix: *"the
idea that the power of a system comes more from the
relationships among programs than from the programs themselves"*. *Pipes* are one of the key mechanisms to do this. In the words of Dennis
Ritchie:

> "One of the most widely admired contribu-
> tions of Unix to the culture of operating sys-
> tems and command languages is the pipe...".[2]

Unix *pipes* are at the heart of McIlroy's
philosophy[3]:

---

[2] "The Evolution Of The Unix Time-Sharing System." *AT&T Bell Laboratories Technical Journal*, vol 63, no. 6 part 2, 1984, pp. 1577-93. -
https://www.bell-labs.com/usr/dmr/www/hist.html

[3] Doug McIlroy, E. N. Pinson, B. A. Tague (8 July 1978). "Unix
Time-Sharing System: Foreword" (PDF). *The Bell System Technical
Journal*. Bell Laboratories. pp. 1902–1903. McIlroy was head of the
Bell Labs Computing Sciences Research Center while Unix was be-
ing written.

1. Make each program do one thing well. To do a new job, build afresh rather than complicate old programs by adding new "features".

2. Expect the output of every program to become the input to another, as yet unknown, program. Don't clutter output with extraneous information. Avoid stringently columnar or binary input formats. Don't insist on interactive input.

3. Design and build software, even operating systems, to be tried early, ideally within weeks. Don't hesitate to throw away the clumsy parts and rebuild them.[4]

4. Use tools in preference to unskilled help to lighten a programming task, even if you have to detour to build the tools and expect to throw some of them out after you've finished using them.

Note the last item: he is talking about *transfer of skill* to machinery (or code in this case).

---

[4] An example of "agile" philosophy long before the term became popular. Other examples abound, most notably the admonitions of C.A. Hoare in his address The Emperor's Old Clothes, (Hoare, Charles Antony Richard. "The Emperor's Old Clothes." *Communications Of The ACM*, vol 24, no. 2, 1981, pp. 75-83.)

Unix was the first implementation of McIlroy's vision. Arguably, the next one was Brad Cox's interchangeable software components (software ICs) in Objective-C, a little bit more than a decade later (the usual time required for adoption of new technology it seems). They most certainly *did* transfer skill; the NextStep libraries transferred a considerable amount of programming skill to a package that could be easily re-used by a programmer with considerably less skill (like me). However, they only worked in Objective-C, and not everybody wanted to use Objective-C. More importantly, it still required *some* skill to use software ICs. NextStep was not yet to the point where *semi-skilled* or *unskilled* labor could use it to assemble a program without help.

Next, in the early 1990's the OMG proposed the CORBA (Common Object Request Broker Architecture) standard, and Microsoft introduced its OLE and COM (Object Linking and Embedding and Component Object Model) models.

CORBA promised to provide out-of-the-box multi-vendor interoperability. It may have been the first credible promise of Mass Produced Software Components because of the number of influential participants in the OMG. Yet despite significant investment by various vendors, it failed to establish a lasting presence for a variety of reasons, mostly centered around its bloated design-by-committee feature. It was just too much of too much. As a result, I would wager there are many more mission critical COBOL-based systems running today than there are CORBA-based ones.

Amusingly, at the time of this writing, the link to "Who is using CORBA already?" on the official OMG "CORBA® BASICS" page[5] leads to *absolutely nothing*. (Bonus points for the old school insistence on using the registered trademark symbol. AT&T would be proud.)

As for Microsoft's Visual Basic component architecture, its language independent successor OLE/DCOM and its spiritual successor .NET, they were resisted by large swaths of the market because they were Microsoft "standards" that in practical terms only worked on Windows, In a world that was rapidly adopting the web as its preferred platform for applications, solutions that did not work on Unix (and later on Linux) servers were not going to succeed. In fact, just as with Objective-C, any solution that depended upon just one operating

---

[5] http://www.omg.org/gettingstarted/corbafaq.htm

I am not sure why, but the page is available in two languages, English and Belorussian.

system, or one language would never succeed across the board.

And I feel that I can very safely predict: the IT industry will never agree to pick just one language or operating system for everyone and everything.

Concurrently with McIlroy, Daniel Teichroew, Professor of Industrial and Operations Engineering at the University of Michigan, had started on what he called the Information System Design and Optimization System project in 1968. Although very interested in programming and automation, he was a statistician and Management Information theorist, not a programmer. His approach was markedly different than McIlroy's.

A well-known and oft used cliché in IT is: "you got what you asked for, not what you needed."

Teichroew's starting point was "the problem" not the code that solved the problem, and he intended to ensure that what one "asked for", was indeed what one "needed".

To remove ambiguity in stating problems (now usually called "requirements"), he developed the Problem Statement Language, the idea being that a formal way of describing requirements would allow for the reliable automated production of code by a Problem Statement Analyzer, a kind of compiler if you will. A traditional compiler converts a 3GL like C or PASCAL to machine language (or sometimes an intermediary language). The Problem Statement Analyzer would convert the Problem Statement Language into a conventional programming language such as C.

Parts of his work, specifically the focus on problem analysis as a means of ensuring successful development, would be picked up by the object-oriented analysis and design researchers. It lives on in the "use case", which is a direct outgrowth of Problem Statement Language. Other parts of his work became the foundation of CASE, which stands for Computer Aided Software Engineering. The idea (which was a good one) was to apply to software the same principles that were successfully used in CAD/CAM (computer-aided design and computer-aided manufacturing).

CASE tools became popular and were widely used for development of mainframe and minicomputer applications in the 1980s and early 1990s. With the decline of the mainframe, the CASE banner was taken up by the Object Management Group as part of the standardization of UML (see Chapter Six) and was embedded into a number of tools such as Rational Rose (it later went through a number of name changes) and Silverrun, both of which still exist.

In 2001 the OMG took another run at promoting these concepts, this time under the banner of Model Driven Architecture (MDA). Under MDA, a *platform independent model* (PIM) was created first to then be machine translated to a *platform specific model* (PSM). This was undoubtedly the right idea, but it went nowhere.

To a carpenter with a hammer, the world is a nail.

You may wonder, if the previous solutions were such great ideas, then why did they never really succeed? Why is the problem of IT Project failures still as present as it ever was?

Because to a carpenter with a hammer, the whole world looks like a nail.

NextStep, COM, .NET, CORBA, CASE, MDA; all had a fatal flaw stemming from a bias shared by almost all programmers, computer scientists and software engineers: to them, *writing code is the alpha and the omega*. The beginning and the end. It is all that there is.

All of the above attempts at software industrialization focused on the "creative" part of development: writing code that "solves a problem" as expressed in a requirement or use case.

I expect that you are now asking yourself: "How could that be a flaw?" Isn't that what programmers do? The answer is no, that is not what they spend most of their time doing. It will probably shock you to learn that enterprise developers are unlikely to spend more than 10% of their time actually writing new code, creating new functions, being creative.

Only the developers working for a FANG, (Facebook, Amazon, Netflix, and Google, remember?) writing compilers, creating advanced image, or language processing, or researching, are spending a lot of time writing algorithms.

Alexander Stepanov, the primary designer and implementer of the C++ Standard Template Library, relays to us[6] that Scott Byer, the

---

[6] Alexander Stepanov: Industrializing Software Development. A keynote address at The First International Conference on Embedded Software and System, Zhejiang University, Hangzhou, P. R. China, December 9, 2004.

architect of Adobe Photoshop, estimates that 90% of developer efforts are dedicated to "glue" and housekeeping tasks such as memory management, scripting, UI management, file I/O, and color management. 10% is spent on "substance".

Stepanov presents the following estimates of how much time is spent on what he deems "substance" for a variety of application types:

- Word processing - 3%,
- Presentation App - 1%,
- Databases - 10%,
- Technical/CAD - 30%,
- Operating System - 1%, and
- Enterprise Application Software - 1%.

From personal experience, these numbers sound just about right to me.

The Story of Me

Let me describe to you a recent programming job I did for a friend. He asked me if I could create a web application that took a list of names and sent each name to a third-party web service which returned a list of results that could be imported into a spreadsheet. It bears mentioning that he *already had* an application that did this, but it was so difficult to use (another failed enterprise IT project) that he asked me for my help in creating a *replacement*. This is a classic example of shadow IT at its best.

Requirements (from his IT department) were that it be written in the Python programming language, and that any libraries or code snippets that I did not write myself used the MIT license (a type of open source license).

I am not a graphic designer, so the best way for me to make sure the app would be pleasant to look at was to search Google and Github and find an MIT licensed UI template. In about an hour I had one I liked, and by the end of the day I had a pretty looking web app that didn't do anything. All the buttons and entry fields were there, they just weren't wired up to anything.

Because my friend's IT department requested that "the code that did the work" be written in Python, I could not do it in JavaScript (a relief to be honest). I searched Github for a Python web server and found very nice one named Bottle. I used the modified UI template as my web content, and by the end of the second day, I had a fully functional Python-based web server with a pretty little UI that promised everything but delivered nothing.

That was a good thing. Because it enabled me to have a discussion with my friend based on an actual on-screen UI. Which forced us to examine some of his assumptions and expectations and clarified some requirements before I wrote any code for them.

To manage the tables of results (before they got exported to the spreadsheet) I used what is likely the most widely used open source library for tables in a web UI: a library named datatables.js. This is where the fun started.

Both datatables.js and the UI template I was using depended upon some CSS and JavaScript code libraries (Bootstrap and JQuery); just not the same ones.

Predictably, datatables.js would not work with the Bootstrap and JQuery that I had already setup for the UI template, and when I used the Bootstrap and JQuery from DataTables, the UI went to hell in a handbasket. It took me the better part of a day to sort out the dependencies, and import versions of Bootstrap and JQuery, and import other CSS and JavaScript in just the right order, so that everything worked the way it should.

It has now been three days and only about two or three *hours* have been spent on the creative work of implementing the UI (what entry fields, buttons etc. and how to lay them out to be useable). The rest has been mostly in getting the different "moving parts" to work with each other.

So far, I have in the way of moving parts:

- Bootstrap CSS library for styling of HTML

- startbootstrap-landing-page template by Blackrock Digital LLC

- jQuery JavaScript library for HTML for DOM manipulation and event handling, using low version to guarantee compatibility with DataTables

- DataTables Plug-in for jQuery to add advanced interaction controls to HTML tables

- Python for server-side scripting

- Bottle, a Python-based WSGI Web Framework

The next step was to decide on the best way to perform the steps of:

1. Sending a line from the list to the web service

2. Getting the result and adding it to a table

3. Loading the table data into datatables.js

There are at least a half a dozen ways to do this. The key challenge or decision is the best way to hand off the data from the Python virtual machine (which does the work of getting the response from the web service), to the JavaScript interpreter in the web browser (which does the work of displaying the datatable).

Do I collect all of the results in Python first and save them as a file, and then read the file into the datatable?

Do I build the datatable line by line in JavaScript with JavaScript calling Python over and over again until it gets nothing (end of list)?

Or is it better for datatables.js to call a handwritten JavaScript function that calls a Python function that returns a JSON object that gets passed back up the chain?

In spite of the fact that datatables.js is one of most widely-used JavaScript libraries in the world, the documentation for many of its functions is a little sketchy, and more than a little inconsistent. Following the documentation, I was simply unable to get it to work even after a few days (as I keep telling you: I am not such a great programmer). I turned to the programmer's best friend: StackExchange. This is a website where programmers ask each other for help. My problem was a common one, and I quickly found an existing question and answer that enabled me to get things working. As usual, it was simply a matter of getting quotation marks, commas, and semi-colons in right places. Really.

I have now spent a full week on this. In addition to the three hours of UI, I have added another two hours of real programming (figuring out how to split up the list into different types of requests).

Out of a full week of work: only five hours spent "writing code" the way Mel[7] did. Thirty-five hours spent getting different libraries to work with each other in much the same way *fitters* used to file away to make parts fit.

I spent another five hours packaging the code with instructions to make sure the IT team could install it without issues, and the IT

---

[7] See *The Story of Mel* in Chapter Two.

department will spend dozens, if not hundreds, of hours monitoring it operationally and applying upgrades and security patches. And this does not even consider the time to be spent on *testing*.

All in all, I have spent at most 5% of my time actually *writing code*.

Hammering a screw

Writing code is clearly *not* the main activity and expense of enterprise IT projects. Trying to automate it is not only difficult; it is a gross misallocation of resources.

This is why Problem Statement Language, CASE and Model Driven Architecture never really gained any popularity: They are the right tools, but for the wrong job.

What we need are tools to automate the repetitive boilerplate and assembly tasks that programmers spend more than half their time doing.

Not only will these tools save time, but they will remove costly manual errors and typos that tired and bored programmers make. Like Bentham's block making robots, they will create a higher quality product.

"Don't worry about people stealing an idea; if it's original, you'll have to shove it down their throats."

~ Howard Aiken

Chapter Fourteen
Wrapping it up

If writing code is not a candidate for automation, then how can IT be industrialized?

To help answer that question, I suggest another look at automobile manufacturing. But first, let's ask: are they comparable? Can a car be compared in complexity to an enterprise IT project? It's a fair question, let's take a look.

A hundred years ago, car manufacture was at a place roughly equivalent to where IT is today: cars were being assembled one by one, by hand, by craftsmen.

Today, automobile production is perhaps the most highly automated and industrialized sector in the world. As I mentioned at the end of Part Three, the automotive industry is the world's largest user of industrial robots.

Apart from the fact that a typical new car already includes up to 100 million lines of code (mostly the non-application type of code), it also has tens of thousands of hardware parts that must be assembled very precisely. The average car has about 30,000 parts including about 12,000 screws and nuts and bolts[1].

What is the equivalent in code? It can't be a line of code. That is too small to make a good comparison, a line of code is even smaller than a screw. What about function points? Those things I said were so complicated that most people cheated and just used a conversion factor on the number of lines of code.

According to the International Function Point Users Group (and no, I did not just make that up[2]), a function point is calculated by first identifying the application components (ILFs, EIFs, EIs, EQs, and EOs) and then counting the RETs and DETs for each of these and using them to weight the application components' complexity. Arriving at the FPs is a *simple* matter of multiplying the application components by the complexity rating and summing them up.

Right? No?

---

[1] http://www.toyota.co.jp/en/kids/faq/d/01/04/, and Walton, Mary. Car: a drama of the American workplace. W.W. Norton, 1999.

[2] I did however, for a very brief moment, think that this organization might have more moxie than I first imagined, when I misread the first word of: "Site matters, press or content: cmc@ifpug.org"

Don't worry, I barely understand it myself.

Fortunately for us, someone else has done the work. Beata Czarnacka-Chrobot of the Warsaw School of Economics has pegged the average cost of developing a function point in the USA at $1,000 USD[3]. Two other papers (Capers Jones' *Software Economics and Function Point Metrics: Thirty years of IFPUG Progress* and Pam Morris's *Functional Size Metrics*) place this estimate on the low end of the spectrum.

Capers Jones uses 10,000 function points as an example of a very large complex project, and the numbers add up because this places the cost of a very large complex project at upwards of $10 million dollars, which is in fact what very large IT projects cost.

There are no definitive studies comparing complexity of software with complexity of automobiles, but with 20,000 (non-screw/nut/bolt) auto parts compared to 10,000 function points it seems that we might be in the same ballpark.

---

[3] Czarnacka-Chrobot, Beata. (2012). What Is the Cost of One IFPUG Method Function Point? – Case Study.

Next let's consider one of the hallmarks of complexity in software: the interdependence and sometime unexpected interactions between one section of code another. Even non-technical people know that fixing one bug can often create several others. As it happens, cars also have similar surprising and unintuitive interactions:

On a Mitsubishi Lancer, the cruise control may stop working if you use LED bulbs in the taillights.

On several models of Volvos turning on the windshield wipers may cause a pulsing or throbbing in the brake pedal.

The Porsche 928 is infamous for strange random electrical gremlins; the car cuts out, the airbag warning lights come on, various motors stop working. The problem: corrosion on one of thirteen ground points. Clean the ground points and tighten them. All problems go away.

Many post-1999 BMWs will not start if the radio is removed. The central computer considers the absence of a radio to be equal to the absence of an engine control module.

These are just a few isolated examples out of many showing parallels between the two. Automobiles have complex interdependence and are prone to unexpected interactions just like software. So far it looks like comparing automobile manufacturing with software development might be justified.

Nonetheless, some people will maintain that writing software is a *creative* process that *cannot* be compared to the mechanical process of assembling a car… and bravo to those people!

That is the question. It is the *right* question to be asking. It is the key to it all.

I happen to agree that there is no comparison between the creative process of writing code and the mechanical process of assembling a car. However, as we saw earlier: before the process of auto assembly starts there is the process of *designing* the car, and I think that there is a very good comparison indeed to be made. The eighteen to thirty-six months spent designing and developing a new car model has *many* parallels to executing a very large IT software project.

Early stages

The very first thing that happens in new car development is the definition of its *purpose*, the needs that it is supposed to fill. What market niche is it competing in? Small and sporty for a young single professional, or roomy and sturdy for a large family? Or perhaps something that will be used on a construction site?

The same thing applies to a new IT project. Who are the users? What business process are they trying to accomplish? Will they use this application every day? Once a month? On a phone, a tablet, a laptop, or all three?

—

The next step for a new car will be to assemble a core team; someone to assume management responsibility for the project, a few experts to create preliminary designs, someone to develop the high-level architecture of the new product, someone to develop the budget.

Ditto for software.

—

A car designer will make freehand sketches intended to convey an overall sense of direction for management approval.

Anyone who has worked on the early stages of a software project has seen something resembling the image below.

—

For both software and cars, very high-level detailed estimates of costs will now be produced and there will be an approval stage before work continues.

—

A car design will go to the packaging design where specifics such as engine type(s), drive train choices, leg room, safety requirements, etc. are finalized.

A software application will be described in detail (from the intended user's point of view) in a business requirements document (BRD).

Development starts

Cars are always modeled. First as scale models in clay and 3D computer programs, but eventually (once the final design has been chosen) as full-sized models. The process continues on to interiors and paint choices as well.

The application might or might not be prototyped. Often it is not, as a result of enforced waterfall project management, but all application development experts agree that it **should**.

—

For a car, master engineers will make final adjustments to the vehicle's design (details about how parts are assembled, and which parts will be used). The final bill of materials for the vehicle will be planned so that real costs can be estimated.

With software, once an application's BRD is finalized, a more detailed estimate (often plus/minus 10%) will be produced by a project manager working with an enterprise architect and lead developer who will make decisions about the technical implementation in order to produce the estimate.

Production

Finally, building the factory tooling, debugging it, and launching full production happens for the car.

BUT…

It is the *tooling and preparation for mass production* that **does not happen** for application development today. Instead, the application is coded, debugged and deployed as a single isolated event, with no thought given to producing the next one.

Conclusion

Some of you will have noticed by now that in spite of the fact that the automotive industry is one of the most highly automated industries in the world, its *design* process is mostly artisanal.

Yes, CAD programs are used, but they do not represent a transfer of skill. You cannot give a CAD program to an unskilled worker and expect to get good industrial engineering as a result. CAD programs are not smart automation, they are just convenient electronic pencils that require a highly skilled engineer to use them. The same is true in programming where an Integrated Development Environment is a powerful time-saving tool, but only in the hands of a skilled developer.

The key thing to take note of is that the automation happens *after* the artisanal design is completed by master craftsmen. It is used to make the *assembly* of automobiles a highly repeatable process that can be accomplished with mostly semi-skilled and unskilled workers.

In *The Story of Me*, just above, I describe how in today's world, it is entirely normal for a programmer or developer's billable hours to be mostly consumed by mechanical assembly tasks, the digital equivalent of filing away at parts to make them fit. I have shown you Alexander Stepanov's numbers that confirm that very few programmers today spend even half of their time working on creative coding tasks that could be compared to the design of a car as opposed to the assembly of a car. They spend their time on *fitting* and *assembly*. This is a shocking waste of valuable time and talent.

If we have anything at all to learn from the automotive industry it is this:

The real opportunity for industrialization of IT *is **not** in writing code*. By now it should be clear to you that coding represents a very small portion of the total effort expended in an IT project.

The lion's share of work and costs *is in the assembly, the glue, the fitting,* the 90% of billable hours that are spent on mechanical assembly tasks, the modern-day equivalent of workers running around the workshop filing away at things to make them fit, and this is where the opportunity is.

To eliminate this fitting, to become truly industrialized, enterprise IT departments will need to develop the same skills and mindset that car manufacturers have. They will need to learn how to separate the design and development from the assembly. They will need to stop artisanally creating each app as though it was completely separate from the last one and start using the valuable brainpower of their best developers to create systems and re-useable code plugins for the assembly of applications out of standardized interchangeable code components.

The FANGs already do this. Google, Facebook, Amazon, all have created sophisticated libraries that are re-used over and over again internally allowing developers to move forward rather than re-invent the wheel.

And new tools are emerging to allow average people to assemble code from components are, however most of them do not have a coherent philosophy of industrialization driving their development. Most of them are written by smart programmers who are simply following their intuitions about how to make app development simpler and more cost effective, and they are making a lot of mistakes. But progress is being made, we will get there eventually, and one last bit of theory will help us understand what good IT industrialization will look like.

Babel

Very few people, including even many professional programmers, have a clear and accurate understanding of how programming languages become machine instructions. It is one of those places where "magic happens".

The best way to understand it is from the bottom up. Fortunately, you have that foundation from reading the first chapters of this book. You learned in "The Metal years: 1950-1960" that programs are stored in a section of memory called the heap and are a series of instructions stored as binary "words". The CPU will step through these instructions one after another, each word triggering a specific CPU operation. One step up from machine code is assembly language which uses human readable mnemonic three letter codes.

We touched upon how assembly (and other languages) get translated into binary machine code. In the case of assembly language, since each three-letter opcode equates to one and only one binary machine opcode the translation is simple and fast. The process is traditionally called assembly, from whence the language gets its name, however assembly is really a form of compilation: the most basic form possible.

Converting from FORTRAN, COBOL, or one of the other early languages is slightly more complex. A FORTRAN instruction like:

```
write ( *, '(a)' ) 'Hello, world!'
```

Or the COBOL instruction:

```
DISPLAY 'Hello world!'.
```

works out to a dozen or more machine instructions (AKA binary opcodes).

The compiler takes a high-level language listing as input, and using a series of rules, converts the high-level instructions into the appropriate series of binary opcodes. This is possible because unlike human languages, computer languages are *formal*.

The idea of formality is a mathematical concept. In a formal language, a limited (*finite*) number of symbols have a rigid syntax that describes exactly how those symbols can be combined to make meaning. You are familiar with arithmetic (e.g. 2 + 2 = 4). Arithmetic uses a formal language. In it 2, 4, +, and = are some of the limited symbols allowed, but they are not interchangeable. The symbol "2" and "4" must always represent values, either to be operated on or to represent results of operations. They are not allowed to be used to represent the operations themselves. Meanwhile the symbols "+" and "-" may never represent values. They *always* represent operations to be performed using symbols representing values. Finally, the "=" symbol is neither an operator, nor a value. It is a *logical* symbol that means that the expression to left of it is numerically identical to the expression on its right.

Natural human language is rarely this clear. In English, the word "equals" may be either a verb, an adjective or a noun and has over a dozen meanings.

Formal mathematical and computer languages are carefully designed to avoid this kind of ambiguity. Words and symbols have very precise meanings that never change. In most cases, an expression or statement will mean one thing and one thing only, and it is for this reason that efficient, accurate, machine translation from any computer language to binary opcodes is possible. But that is not all. There is a concept in programming known as "Turing Completeness". The term comes from the famous English mathematician and computer scientist Alan Turing. To quote Wikipedia:

> "In colloquial usage, the terms "Turing complete" or "Turing equivalent" are used to mean that any real-world general-purpose computer or computer language can approximately simulate the computational aspects of any other real-world general-purpose computer or computer language."

In other words, as long as a language is Turing complete (and every major programming language is):

Any programming language has the potential to be reliably translated to another programming language.

In practice, this happens all the time. If you look at a web page, it is happening right in front of your eyes. The browser is translating the HTML into the DOM, which is an XML-like model in memory. As well, the CSS in the web page you are looking at was more than likely written in SASS or LESS which are language extensions that pre-compile to CSS the same way Objective-C pre-compiles to C. And it is becoming more likely every day that the JavaScript in the page you are looking at was written in CoffeeScript or TypeScript which are... you guessed it: language extensions that pre-compile to JavaScript the same way Objective-C pre-compiles to C.

In spite of the differences that the average programmer will draw between compiling and interpreting, or between static compilation and just-in-time compilation (JIT), the reality is that all languages – every single one – eventually compiled down to machine code, all that changes is when the compilation occurs, how many steps there are, and whether or not the compiled code can be changed or optimized while the code is running.

Pre-compiling, or trans-piling is a normal everyday occurrence in the programming world. Modern programming would be impossible without multiple layers of compilation. It is simply that most programmers are not really aware of it happening, or just don't think about it that way.

The machines that build other machines

The reason why I really want you to understand this is because of the importance of *transfer of skill*. I have been building my case to you that all of the really big advances in productivity come from the transfer of skill from a human to a machine, and compilers are the first example of how that is possible in IT.

Remember from Part One that when compilers first appeared, master programmers did not like or trust them, feeling that human programmers would always do a better job of optimizing machine language. But over time, so much *skill* was transferred to compilers that modern compilers will consistently generate much better machine language than almost any human programmer.

It may have occurred to some of you by now that maybe a compiler is a robot. By my definition, it is.

There have been four order of magnitude advances in programming productivity since the beginning in 1949:

- Compilers (*robots*)
- Class Libraries (interchangeable parts)
- Virtual Machines with JIT (*robots*)
- Open Source Libraries (*interchangeable parts*)

For robots to be successful, it is important to automate the right things. Things that require skill but are repetitive and error-prone, not creative things that are better handled by humans. In the programming world, the robots that were successful are compilers (remember: JIT stands for Just-In-Time compilation).

What a compiler does is a perfect candidate for automation: a highly repetitive and tedious task that nonetheless requires a very high level of skill and attention. The kind of task where mistakes are easy to make. Whenever you see this kind of task being performed by humans, you will also see quality problems. Mistakes made by bored, tired people.

"Computers are like Old Testament gods; lots of rules and no mercy."

~ Joseph Campbell

As you have seen, the reality of programming is that there is a tremendous amount of this type of repetitive, non-creative work that goes into making an application that will run on a computer. The first compilers came about because people like Grace Hopper realized that it simply did not make sense for a human to write out the dozen opcodes for printing a line to screen. It needs to be done hundreds or thousands of times for one program. If a human would write them all out by hand then then there are hundreds or thousands of opportunities for a mistake to occur. And it is not a function that requires human ingenuity, there is simply no good reason why one should not use a robot that converts the word DISPLAY to the required opcodes.

Another good example is sorting. Programs are constantly sorting data, it is just something that happens *a lot*. Believe it or not there are over 40 different ways to sort a collection or set of data. Some work best with integers, other work better for strings of letters, some are very fast with large sets, but not so great on smaller sets and others are the reverse.

Very few modern programmers pay attention to which one of the 40 sorting algorithms is being used when they sort something. They just type "sort", and the compiler does the rest for them. Faster than a human ever could, the compiler analyses the amount and type of data to be sorted and then uses rules to apply the optimal sorting type. It might be that 5% or 10% of the time, a master programmer could do a *slightly* better job of picking, but over 90% of the time the compiler does a *much* better job. So again, it is not something that absolutely requires human ingenuity, there is no good reason why one should not use a robot to do it.

The time has come for another robot. This one will automate or eliminate the following tedious, repetitive, and error prone jobs:

- Controlling the logical progression or flow from one screen to another,
- Making sure that the data to be presented and captured are accessible to the code no matter which system they are on,
- Connecting that data to a Designer's tool so the application can be designed with real-world data instead of *Lorem Ipsum*.
- Reproducing a designer's layouts pixel by pixel,
- Guessing at how the designer would like to have those designs adapt to changing screen sizes (*and being wrong about it, triggering cycles of re-work*),
- Guessing at interactions based on pencil scrawls on wireframe printouts and photos

of whiteboards (*and being wrong about it, triggering cycles of re-work*),

- Writing boilerplate integration code,
- Compiling and testing every time a design changes,
- Deploying code to test machines where designers and business owners can play around with the app and decide that what they asked for was not what they wanted… *triggering cycles of re-work.*

The new compiler that we need is a *Design Compiler*, and the new language it will translate from must be an *Application Modeling Language or AML.*

An AML must able to completely describe an application in a way that is not tied to any particular programming language.

If you remember all the way back to the beginning of the book, I said that an application is different from other kinds of programs and programming in two ways: a) it has a user interface, which b) allows the user to interact with the applications data.

At a conceptual level any app for any computer or device can be described with just six basic concepts:

1. Processes, sometimes called "flows", or "customer journeys".
2. Steps within the processes.
3. The data that is required for each step; either data we want to present to the user, or data we want to collect from the user, or both.
4. The specific means of presenting the steps to the user. In a multi-channel world, this could be anything from a laptop screen to a watch to a telephone or a smart speaker like Amazon Alexa Echo.
5. The "elements" in each unit of presentation. An element can be existing data (one piece or a whole list), a place for new data entry, or a control. A button or a recognized voice command is an example of a control element.
6. And finally: interactions. Any element has the potential of triggering some interaction, either navigation (e.g. go to next step) or some function that exists "behind" the user interface such as validating the username and password, or getting the user's account balance, or making a certain data entry field become visible only if a previous field has been filled in.

An AML would provide a way to specify these six parts of an application and how they interact with each other, and with external apps (a reality in almost every app these days).

This is the vision of Teichroew's Problem Statement Language and CASE, or the OMG's Model Driven Architecture, writ large. If you remember, as I introduced you to these two efforts, I commented that they were trying to do exactly the right thing, but focusing on the wrong part of the problem (the creative writing of code as opposed to the repetitive "gluing together" or fitting of code).

AML should not be manually written by humans. It should be generated by another kind of robot: the visual studio. There are many such drag and drop coding systems on the market today. Perhaps hundreds. They provide a visual interface where a designer can drag and drop and position elements on screen, and then they convert that design into code.

Most of the ones available today generate HTML, CSS and JavaScript. This is okay but not great. HTML and CSS are primarily *document description* languages. At the risk of stating the obvious: apps are not documents. That is why modern web sites and apps always contain some JavaScript. It is needed to provide the interactivity that satisfies items 1,2, and 6 from the conceptual definition of an app I provided above.

A visual studio that produced AML would be infinitely superior. AML does not force the application into a particular paradigm. AML has the advantage that it can be given to a *design compiler* and converted to *any* target platform, even non-screen devices and Internet of Things. This is not true of applications described in HTML, CSS and JavaScript.

The design compiler takes the description of an app in AML, and trans-piles it into source code in *any* other language from JavaScript to FORTRAN.

An obscure reference to *A Story About 'Magic'*[4]

I know this sounds like fantasy to many people reading this, but I know it is possible, because I have seen it and used it. It exists today.

---

[4] http://catb.org/jargon/html/magic-story.html

The journey which led me to write this book started when one of the programmers on my team (Robert Leclair, to whom I owe a lot) suggested I look at a product written by a Finnish programmer named Pauli Olavi Ojala.

I fell completely in love with what I saw, and then spent the next two years trying to explain to everyone around me why I was so excited. A few people got it right away, but very, very, few.

Most people struggled to make sense of what I was saying, and all of those discussions forced me to slow down and consciously explain many things which were purely intuitive to me after more than three decades of pursuing my craft. The result is this book.

Neonto is the product that Pauli created, and with my own eyes I have seen it trans-pile from AML to languages from JavaScript to C, and for platforms from web browsers to phones, glasses, watches, and smart speakers.

Is IT Industrialization really a thing?

I have seen the industrialization of IT in real life happening now. I am not a great thinker who dreamt all of this up when an app fell on my head. I'm just a guy who is getting a little long in the tooth, who has seen a lot of things, and can put two and two together because of that.

Someone once said to me that I know where all the bodies are buried, and it is true that after thirty years in the trenches, working at both executive levels and way down in the projects where the rubber meets the road, I know the dirty secrets of enterprise IT better than most. I know what *doesn't* fix IT project failure better than most. And I know that I have seen the future. It is here today although only a few people recognize it or understand it. However, it is only a matter of time.

Nobody is exempt from history. There are no special rules for programmers. App development *will* eventually go the way of all other industrial production in this world, with product design and development separated from mass-production.

With a design compiler we separate the work of the developer from the work of the designer. We no longer need more developers to create more apps. If this sounds wrong to you: remember that once upon a time people believed that it was impossible to write programs without assembly language programmers. Today we no longer need assembly language programmers on every development team just to be able to write an application.

In auto manufacturing, when you want more cars, you do not hire more designers and engineers.[5] You ramp up production line capacity instead. However, enterprise IT is going about things in the opposite way. Developers write and assemble apps in a single process, in collaboration with designers. There is no separation. If you want more apps, you need more developers.

And there simply are not enough developers to go around. Every large enterprise has a long list of IT projects that would have helped the business but were put on hold or were cancelled because there just was not enough money to hire more developers, or just not enough developers even though the money was there.

And in spite of what a few bright-eyed idealists would like you to believe, *not everybody wants to, or is even able to, learn how to program well.*

I will quote the venerable Dijkstra:

---

[5] Good thing too. There are not enough designers and engineers in the world to produce 160,000 cars a day by hand.

Don't blame me for the fact that competent programming, as I view it as an intellectual possibility, will be too difficult for the average programmer, you must not fall into the trap of rejecting a surgical technique because it is beyond the capabilities of the barber in his shop around the corner.

~ Edsger Dijkstra

We no longer accept that barbers try their hand at surgery from time to time[6], so why do we accept marginally competent (or completely incompetent) programmers writing code that we depend upon daily?

Why? Because very few executives (and virtually *no* HR people) really know how to tell the difference between a good programmer and a not-good one, and nobody really sees the disastrous results until it is way too late.

The world needs to swallow a bitter pill: many of the people programming today are not good enough. They will never be good enough. They simply should not be programming.

Society has no trouble accepting that not everyone can be a jet pilot, or a surgeon, or a

---

[6] Once upon a time we *did* accept this.

good schoolteacher, or a cop or a musician. Some people simply do not have the aptitude or ability. Yet there are those that would have you believe that anyone can code. That we should teach *every child* to code. That is just straight up delusional. Would we try to teach every child how to fly a plane or perform an appendectomy?

Business must accept that there is no new cohort of millions of master programmers about to magically appear and allow IT to *finally* meet the demand for new business apps. Business cannot reasonably expect *more* (of the same) out of IT. But it can demand *different*.

The punchline

A small number of good developers can create interchangeable software parts for less talented programmers to use (the same way a small number of assembly language programmers can create a good compiler for less talented programmers to use) and put them into a tool that is accessible to designers. Something that looks like all of the design tools they use today. Tools like this exist today, and Neonto is not the only one.[7]

Another point that I mentioned early on in the book (Chapter Three), and promised to return to, is the fact that smaller programs are easier to write, have fewer bugs, make it easier to find the bugs that are there, and are easier to maintain. I gave the example that if you clean your kitchen a little bit every day, it is a lot easier than trying one big cleanup every month. I explained that the Unix philosophy of writing smaller programs, that rely upon other previously written (and tested and debugged) programs, is more productive than writing big world-domination type programs. And let us not forget that McIlroy, who created the Unix philosophy, had a bigger vision in mind: a vision of interchangeable software components, as did Brad Cox after him, and that I said I believed that the vision failed to materialize because the solutions were language specific and we will never see the day when all programmers work with the same language.

The technology finally exists with which to make these components in a way that is not language dependent. One plugin can contain

---

[7] Neonto *is* however, the only one that generates AML that can be trans-piled by a design compiler into source code of any language. This is why I became a shareholder.

implementations of its function and logic in as many languages as desired.

Any journeyman programmer can write small blocks of code that are reusable in the context of a well-defined framework. Any master programmer can design such a framework. If we ask them to.

However, nobody's asking them. Instead, enterprise IT departments are asking programmers to spend their precious time wrestling with the same problems, over and over again, like the movie Groundhog Day with programmers instead of a TV news team.

The massive duplication that I have already told you about coupled with mind numbing repetitive "glue" tasks, leads to an unimaginable level of wasted effort on issues such as the ones on the following list which was provided to me by a solution architect and lead developer with whom I worked at a $10B company providing development services to a $30B company:

Software Development Issues in Multi-Vendor environments

The following problem areas are common to the more complex development environments where there are multiple vendors

working simultaneously on various components of a large enterprise application (eg: multiple tier consumer web portal).

Simultaneous Updates

Inadequate strategy for the version control system for code branching/merging/release(s) may result in several people changing the same module and some of these updates being lost, resulting in additional time lost with defining a rollback strategy, reconfiguration.

Configuration Clashes

Different development teams (i.e. from different vendors) may establish different configuration requirements for shared aspects of the delivery environment. When the code is finally merged just before deployment there may be issues establishing the final correct configuration.

Unavailable Resources

Different parts of the development teams need access to key areas of the system(s), but there are not enough people with the knowledge and experience of these areas to support the simultaneous development effort.

Extending Scope (Scope Creep)

Sometimes the developers realize that it would be "easy" to do this/and that, as well as the things originally requested. More often than not, the business users think of more "core" features the longer the development goes on.

New Application Context

An application (i.e. function/subroutine/assembly/ caching layer app, etc.) which works perfectly well in one context is used (because "we know it works") in a slightly different context (changed workload, different HW, SW patches, etc.). Some of the original assumptions no longer hold true, and the application now fails sometimes - often in subtle ways which are difficult to spot.

Uncovering Old Problems

An application which appeared to work perfectly in one context is used correctly, but with different data, loading patterns, etc. in a new environment. Errors which were always present but did not manifest themselves will suddenly come to light.

If large companies took the amount of time, money, and effort wasted on this kind of duplication, and spent only one quarter of that amount on creating internal no-code tools that could be used by Business Analysts and User Interface Designers, the list of problems described above would disappear. For new systems.

Old legacy systems would continue to perpetuate the project-based chaos factory until they were replaced once and for all. And although very few business leaders would keep the kind of car known as a lemon, a car that was constantly breaking down, needing one part after another to be replaced or repaired, never working completely reliably, almost all business leaders of large corporations are doing exactly this with legacy IT systems.

I must say however, not all legacy systems. Mainframe applications written in FORTRAN or COBOL are still in use today, and they are surprisingly easy and inexpensive to maintain. They were written at time when code craftsmanship was higher. The programmers who work on them today know what they are doing. The hacks and quacks of today code in Java and JavaScript, not FORTRAN. FORTRAN applications are maintained by *real* programmers. As the saying goes: "if you think that hiring an expert is expensive, wait until you see how much costs to hire an amateur!"

When you read about some huge IT failure in the papers, with tens or hundreds of millions of dollars wasted and still no working system, it will be a system written sometime in the last twenty years, and I can pretty much guarantee you that it was written in Java or .NET.

I am not blaming Java for the fact that so many bad programs have been written in it, we must not confuse correlation with causation. As I said earlier: languages come in and out of fashion with each generation of programmers. And I explained the reasons for Java becoming so popular. So, it was Java's bad luck to have been used (or rather, misused) for so much atrociously bad development. It was just unfortunate timing.

These failing applications were written in an era when, corporate processes, committee decision making, and above all, project management and outsourcing culture, prevented the kind of architectural purity and programmer discipline that would be required to avoid the current nightmare of simultaneous updates, configuration clashes, resource scarcity, and subtle logic bombs that my former colleague wrote about just above.

As Brookes proposed: there is no silver bullet. I am not advocating new technology that will magically solve all problems with no effort or difficult change. I am advocating using existing technology differently. I am advocating organizational change that is frightening at many levels. Not only is the security blanket of project management going to be difficult to give up, but to be able to make the organizational transition from a *project management culture* to a *production culture*, business needs to face the ugly and frightening prospect of retiring and replacing legacy systems that were built "like an Egyptian pyramid". This is so frightening because in many cases, nobody can claim to completely understand what the old system does. Replacing it with a new one confronts managers with the fear that the new system will miss some critical feature. That no one will notice its missing until the old system is shut off and it's too late.

The fact that we have this fear at all should tell us everything we need to know about how fragile existing systems are and how badly they need to be replaced before we dig ourselves any deeper. Imagine if we were afraid to buy a new car, because we couldn't be sure it would do all the things that the old car did!

Time to stop talking and start doing

I have told you what went wrong. I have told you what we need to do to fix it. In this last few pages I am going to try to provide the *motivation* to do it.

Change is hard for humans. We do not like it. We very often choose to live with serious problems rather than face the discomfort of changing the causes of those problems. I believe I am a realist, not an idealist. I understand

and accept that people need motivation. They need a *reason* to do things, and I will do my best to provide that.

For the CFO

You come first, because of fiduciary duty. I understand that your decisions are constrained by regulators and shareholders.

* Moving to this new way of doing things will be less expensive. Interchangeable software parts are *reusable* software parts. Right now, you are paying developers to write the same code over and over again. You don't believe me? Have a frank, off the record, talk with a lead dev. Not a CIO, not a VP, not an IT Director. They all have something to hide. In fact, make it clear to the dev lead that nothing will get back to the bosses. In fact: don't you do it. Get someone you trust, someone good with people, someone low on the totem pole, to do it. You'll see.

* Interchangeable software parts are 100% CapEx. They are for *reuse*, you can't get much clearer than that.

* Preparing for audit is trivial. The people who are doing the OpEx activities are nowhere near your dev team. They are consumers of the software just as surely as if

they were using SalesForce. Industrialized IT turns your devs into an arm's length provider of reusable software components that clearly have no connection to specific one-time implementations, graphic design, documentation, training, change management, or any of those other *operational expenses* in your projects. Audit related costs will plummet.

- Last, but not least; your shareholders might be reading this book. They might be asking themselves *right now* if your company is one of those companies wasting millions of *their* dollars on IT project failures that could be avoided by applying tried and true industrial techniques to the production of applications.

For the CEO

You come next, because rank has its privileges.

- Moving to this new way of doing things will get you to market faster. Interchangeable software parts are *reusable* software parts, but they are also *debugged* parts. Applications that are assembled out of interchangeable software parts are for practical purposes *already debugged*. The first time a plugin is used in an app some bugs will come up, but by time that same plugin is used in its tenth app, its twentieth app, you can be pretty darn sure all the bugs are out. You can also be sure that your teams know how to use it right and how to use it fast. Industrialized IT is fast, just like pumping one more car off the assembly line.

For the CIO or CTO

Be a thought leader. Take *business* responsibility by solving business problems. Don't wait for the villagers to come waving pitchforks. Get out in front of this.

- Maybe not this year, or even next year, but soon enough, Industrialized IT will be a thing. When that day comes, any IT department that clings to artisanal production will find themselves in the same position newspapers are in today. Do yourself a favor; talk to a newspaper publisher or editor. These guys were feeling pretty smug not too long ago. They had an answer for everything. They knew what time it was. They were *on top of it*.

- Do yourself a second favor: don't misread me. I'm not saying all programmers will be replaced by automation. That's ridiculous. Remember what I said about car production: the magic is in the separation of design from mass-production. You still need your programmers. You just won't need the *bad ones* anymore. You still need the good ones to build your robots and your interchangeable software parts that make it possible for BSAs and Graphic Designers with no coding skills to make apps on their own.

For the Programmer

Look forward to this future. It is the only hope you have of being *truly* agile. Writing interchangeable software parts allows you to do what most developers dream of:

- You are building a real product, not yet another crappy project.
- You will no longer need to get involved in the endless back and forth between the business, the Business Analysts, and the Designers. Your job is done when you deliver a plugin.
- Your code is well encapsulated; you are protected from other developer's mistakes! They can't break your build.
- The bad and mediocre developers are going far far away from you.
- Interchangeable software parts usually take days or weeks to deliver. Too short for *project management*! Goodbye project

managers. The *only* way to deliver something that takes only a few days to code is Agile.

- If you have trouble believing that you can truly "walk away" from end to end application integration and testing, think about compilation: do you manually inspect and validate every line of assembly code, and profile it to make sure it is optimized? No? Well, we used to have to do that back in the old days. Now we do not. The design compiler will evolve to the same level, where one day it will make no more sense for a programmer to look at the end-to-end integration than it would for you to read each line of assembly.

For the BA, BSA, and Designer

Do I really have to say anything to convince you? Okay here is the obvious:

- Iterate UI and UX as often as you want with no developer-imposed delays.
- Preview your apps in actual production code instead of simulations that are never exactly what you get in production.
- Design with real, live data from staging or testing back-ends. Catch edge cases and corner cases before acceptance testing

For the Shareholder

Get real profits, not paper profits.

- CFOs hide the millions of wasted IT dollars by balancing the money coming out of the bank with an entry in assets instead of expenses. But it is still real money coming out of the bank account, and the assets are pretty much imaginary. It is not like some other company would pay hard cash to buy the broken payroll system that is on the books as an asset.

- IT expenses are, at the very least, *twice as much* as they should be, imagine all that money *remaining* in the bank account. Liquidity will always be a far sight better than some intangible asset. Cash is king.

Final words

I have encountered tremendous resistance to these ideas from most IT professionals I discuss this with. It reminds me a lot of the resistance I met from the newspaper industry in 2008 when I tried to convince them that the world had changed around them, and they needed to come up with a new business model – fast.

Sticking their heads in the sand did not work for the newspapers, and it will not work any better for IT professionals. A change is coming, whether they agree with it or not.

Before I leave you, I want to thank you for your attention, and your time. I am trying to make a difference with this book. I hope it made a difference for you.